FAITHFULLY FIERCE

SHERI ANN ALPEROVICH

COPYRIGHT © 2024
Sheri Ann Alperovich

All rights are reserved. No part of this book may be reproduced, distributed, or transmitted in any form or by any means, including photocopying, recording, or other electronic or mechanical methods, without the prior written permission of the author, except in the case of brief quotations embodied in critical reviews and certain other noncommercial uses permitted by copyright law. For permission requests, write to the author at the address provided in the acknowledgments section of this book.

Printed in the United States of America
First Printing Edition, 2024

Acknowledgments

First and foremost, I want to thank God for the countless blessings He's poured into my life—the strength, courage, wisdom, and experiences that have shaped me and led me to write this book. And, jokingly, thank you for giving me the time to do it! To my husband, Alex, and my boys, Aaron, Jacob, and Ethan—thank you for making me a mother and filling my life with endless love and encouragement. You've given me the space to reach my goals, and more than that, you've allowed me to chase my dreams.

I am beyond blessed to have each one of you by my side, and I love you with all my heart. Thank you to my mother, who has been my guide and my rock. Your faith and the way you live a God-centered life have shaped me into the woman I am today. Your love and example have laid the foundation for everything I do, and for that, I am forever grateful.

And to my dear Aunt Jeanie—thank you for teaching me how to pray and for the daily devotions that inspired me to write my own. Your example of faith and strength has left a lasting imprint on my heart. You've shown me the power of prayer and its ability to lift, comfort, and inspire. This book wouldn't be possible without the seeds you planted in my life.

With love and gratitude,

Sheri

Contents

Acknowledgments III

Dedication VI

Author's Note VII

Introduction IX

Chapter One: Juggling the Chaos: Prayers for Moms, Career Women, and Homemakers 1

Chapter Two: Leading with Grace: Prayers for Women in Leadership and Life 40

Chapter Three: Building Dreams: Prayers for Entrepreneurs and Creative Visionaries 78

Chapter Four: Starting Strong: Prayers for Women Beginning New Chapters ... 114

Chapter Five: Finding Purpose: Prayers for Women Embracing Life Transitions 149

Chapter Six: Serving with Heart: Prayers for Helpers, Healers, and Professionals 185

Chapter Seven: Navigating Relationships Beyond Family 220

Dedication

To my family, whose love and support have been my foundation, and to my friends, who have walked alongside me through every season. To the readers, may this book be a source of hope, encouragement, and a reminder of God's unwavering grace in your life.

In His Love,

Sheri Ann ♡

Author's Note

Faithfully Fierce was born out of a simple desire: to bring hope, encouragement, and God's love into the everyday lives of busy women. Life can be overwhelming, with countless demands pulling us in every direction. In those moments, it's easy to forget how deeply God cares for us and how fiercely He fights for our hearts.

This book is a collection of prayers, reflections, and truths that have carried me through my own struggles and triumphs. It's a reminder that no matter where you are in your journey—whether you're navigating joy, sorrow, or the in-between—God is with you. He sees you, He loves you, and He longs to meet you exactly where you are.

My hope is that these words will inspire you to seek Him daily, even in the smallest moments. Let this be your time to connect with the One who knows you fully and loves you completely. May you find strength in your faith, courage in your prayers, and joy in the knowledge that you are never alone.

Thank you for allowing *Faithfully Fierce* to be a part of your journey. It is my prayer that it blesses your heart as much as it has blessed mine to write it.

With love and faith,

Sheri Ann Alperovich

Introduction

Welcome to Faithfully Fierce!

Hi, friends. I'm so glad you're here. To start this journey together, let's just say life can be full and beautiful, but let's be honest—it's also overwhelming at times. Finding time for God can feel like just another thing on the to-do list between work, family, and everything else pulling at you. I get it. As a working mom of three boys, I've had plenty of days where I've wondered, *how am I supposed to fit prayer into all of this?*

But here's the truth I've discovered: prayer isn't about perfection and doesn't have to be long or formal. It's about inviting God into your day, wherever you are—whether packing lunches, sitting through a meeting, or tackling a mountain of laundry. It's about living life *with* Him in the moments that make up your day.

This book was written for you—the working woman, the mother, the homemaker—because I know how easy it is to feel disconnected from God in the busyness of life. Inside, you'll find prayers tailored to the unique situations you face daily, designed to guide and encourage you while reminding you that you're never alone.

Why Faithfully Fierce?

This journey started with two incredible women in my life: my mom and my Aunt Jeanie. My mom taught me how to talk to God like a friend, weaving little conversations with Him into the rhythm of her day. My Aunt Jeanie showed me the power of consistency through her daily devotions, which she shared with our big Italian family.

When my aunt faced overwhelming challenges during my uncle's illness and could no longer write her devotions, I stepped in to help. I started writing prayers and sending them to her and our family. Soon, I began sharing them with friends, who then shared them with others. Before I knew it, these prayers had taken on their own life. My pastor friend started posting them to his ministry page, and another friend included them in his ministry's daily newsletter.

The responses were incredible. People would tell me how the prayers were exactly what they needed to hear that day, how they felt like a personal message from God. That's when I realized the impact these simple, heartfelt prayers could have—and it planted the seed for *Faithfully Fierce*. This book is the result of that journey.

The 3-Minute Prayer Challenge

I know your time is precious, so I created the *3-Minute Prayer Challenge*. It's a practical, no-pressure way to connect with God every day. You don't need hours or a quiet space—just three intentional minutes. Here's how it works:

1. **Reflection (1 Minute):** Pause and ask yourself a simple question: *What blessing can I thank God for today?* or *What challenge can I hand over to Him right now?* This step is about noticing where God is moving in your life.

2. **Scripture (1 Minute):** Read a short Bible verse and let it resonate with you. Whisper it to yourself throughout the day, or let it guide your thoughts back to Him.

3. **Personal Prayer (1 Minute):** Talk to God in your own words. Share your joys, struggles, and gratitude. It's as simple as saying, "Lord, thank You for this day. Please help me stay calm in this moment."

To help you practice this, I've included a *3-Minute Prayer Challenge* at the end of each chapter. These challenges tie directly to the prayers and scriptures in each chapter, allowing you to incorporate this practice into your day. By the end of this book, you'll feel confident praying for yourself, writing prayers for others, and inviting God into every part of your life.

Why This Matters

Friend, this journey isn't about doing life perfectly—it's about doing life with God. As you move through these pages, I hope you'll feel His presence in your everyday moments, from the mundane to the monumental. You'll discover He's always near, ready to guide and encourage you.

Let's walk this road together. When you finish this book, I hope you'll feel empowered to pray boldly, write prayers that speak to your heart and others, and live every moment with Him.

So, let's get started. You don't have to do life alone—God is with you, and I'm cheering you on every step of the way.

Chapter One:
Juggling the Chaos: Prayers for Moms, Career Women, and Homemakers

This set of prayers is a heartfelt companion for mothers navigating the challenges of balancing work and family. Each prayer addresses a specific need, from moments of gratitude to requests for patience and strength, reflecting the emotional journey of motherhood.

These prayers serve as a resource to turn to in various situations:

- **Gratitude and Provision** – For appreciating the ability to provide for the family despite sacrifices.

- **Patience and Calm** – When hectic schedules strain patience, seek peace and the grace to respond with love.

- **Strength and Resilience** – To face challenges with composure and rely on faith during tough times.

- **Guidance in Decisions** – This is for wisdom in making choices that impact family life and balancing career and home.
- **Mindfulness and Presence** – To savor moments with loved ones, shifting focus from tasks to family.

Mothers can turn to these prayers in moments of stress, guilt, gratitude, or reflection. The benefits are profound: fostering peace, reconnecting with faith, building resilience, and finding clarity in life's daily demands. Each prayer offers a moment to pause, realign priorities, and embrace the journey of motherhood with renewed strength and purpose.

1. Gratitude for the Ability to Provide for Family

Heavenly God, thank You for the gift of provision. As a working mother, there are days when I feel torn between the responsibilities of my job and my role at home. I struggle with guilt—guilt for the moments missed with my children, for the nights I come home late, and for the days when I'm just too tired to give more. But, Lord, I know that the work I do is a way to provide for my family, to ensure they have all they need, and to set an example of perseverance and hard work. Help me find joy in my role, not just as a mother but as a provider. When I feel stretched thin, it reminds me of the blessings that come from my efforts—the roof over our heads, the meals on our table, and the security we share. May my work be a testament to Your provision, and may I serve my family well through it all. Amen.

Scripture:

"And God is able to bless you abundantly, so that in all things at all times, having all that you need, you will abound in every good work."

– 2 Corinthians 9:8

2. Patience Amidst Hectic Schedules

Lord, You see my day-to-day life—the early morning wake-ups, scrambling to get everyone ready and out the door, rushing to work, and then coming home to homework, dinner, and endless to-do lists. It often feels like a race with no finish line in sight, and my patience wears thin. I snap at my children when they take too long, or I feel overwhelmed when everything doesn't go according to plan. God, I need Your Peace to calm my anxious heart. Help me slow down to remember that having a messy house or a late dinner is okay as long as love is in our home. Grant me the patience to handle my children's needs without frustration, to meet my work demands with grace, and to see each moment—no matter how hectic—as an opportunity to reflect Your love and patience to those around me. Amen.

Scripture:

"Be completely humble and gentle; be patient, bearing with one another in love."

— **Ephesians 4:2**

3. Strength to Face Challenges with Grace

God, there are days when I feel I have nothing left to give. Juggling work, family, and my own needs is exhausting, and sometimes I feel like I'm failing at all of them. When I face a demanding project at work, I feel like I'm neglecting my family. And when a child is sick or struggling, it's hard to focus on anything else. Lord, I need Your strength to stand firm when I feel weak to approach challenges not with frustration or defeat, but with grace. Help me handle criticism with an open heart, handle disappointments with faith, and face each Challenge with a sense of purpose. Remind me that I am enough, not because I do everything perfectly, but because You are with me, giving me grace upon grace. Let my strength come from You so I can uplift those around me—especially my family. Amen.

Scripture:

"But he said to me, 'My grace is sufficient for you, for my power is made perfect in weakness.' Therefore, I will boast all the more gladly about my weaknesses so that Christ's power may rest on me."

– 2 Corinthians 12:9

4. Wisdom in Making Decisions That Impact the Family

Dear Lord, so many choices rest on my shoulders—decisions about my career path, childcare, finances, and the daily needs of my family. I often feel overwhelmed by the weight of making the "right" decision and am afraid of the long-term effects they might have. Should I work more hours for the financial benefit, or be home more for the emotional one? Should I invest in my career development now or save that energy for my family? Please, Lord, I need Your wisdom to navigate these choices. Help me see what truly matters and not be swayed by guilt, fear, or societal pressures. Open my heart to Your guidance so that I can make decisions with a clear mind and a peaceful heart, knowing that You are guiding my family toward the future You have planned for us. Amen.

Scripture:

"If any of you lacks wisdom, you should ask God, who gives generously to all without finding fault, and it will be given to you."

– James 1:5

5. Peace in the Present Moment

God, I confess that my mind is constantly racing—thinking about tomorrow's schedule, next week's deadlines, and the never-ending to-do list. I struggle to simply be. Even when I am physically present with my family, my mind is often elsewhere, planning, worrying, or feeling guilty about what's left undone. I miss the joy of my child's laughter, the comfort of an evening with my spouse, and the simple beauty of everyday life. Help me find Peace in the present, Lord. Let me lay my worries at Your feet and be fully engaged in the moments that matter most. When I'm playing with my children, let me enjoy their smiles. When I'm sitting down to dinner, let me savor every bite and every word spoken. Help me to see that Your Peace isn't just a lack of chaos but a sense of contentment no matter what's happening around me. Teach me to be present, to find joy in today, and to trust that You hold all of my tomorrows. Amen.

Scripture:

"Peace I leave with you; my Peace I give you. I do not give to you as the world gives. Do not let your hearts be troubled and do not be afraid."

– **John 14:27**

6. Balancing Self-Care and Care for Others

God, thank You for giving me the heart to care deeply for my family and serve them with love. But Lord, I admit I often neglect my own needs in my pursuit to care for others. I feel guilty for taking time to rest, to exercise, or even to enjoy a quiet moment. I need Your help to find balance—to see self-care not as a luxury but as a way to be the best version of myself for those I love. Remind me that even Jesus took time away from the crowds to rest and pray. Help me create space to be replenished, to renew my strength, and to care for my body, mind, and spirit. Guide me in establishing healthy boundaries and give me the grace to take care of myself without feeling selfish. Amen.

Scripture:

"Do you not know that your bodies are temples of the Holy Spirit, who is in you, whom you have received from God? You are not your own."

– 1 Corinthians 6:19

7. Letting Go of Guilt for Not "Doing It All"

Dear Lord, there is so much pressure to be everything to everyone—a devoted mom, a successful professional, a loving wife, and a great friend. I often feel like I'm failing, like I'm not doing enough or being enough. But You remind me that I am not called to be perfect; I am called to be faithful. Help me to let go of the guilt that weighs me down when I can't do it all. Show me how to set realistic expectations and priorities and forgive myself when falling short. Let me find comfort in Your grace, knowing that my worth is not measured by my productivity or my ability to meet every demand. Help me see that I am already enough in You and that I am loved just as I am. Amen.

Scripture:

"But he said to me, 'My grace is sufficient for you, for my power is made perfect in weakness.' Therefore, I will boast all the more gladly about my weaknesses so that Christ's power may rest on me."

– 2 Corinthians 12:9

8. Joy in the Small Moments of Motherhood

Lord, thank You for the beautiful gift of motherhood. In the midst of the busy days and the sleepless nights, it's easy to miss the small moments that make this journey so precious. Help me to find joy in the little things—the laughter of my children, the warmth of a hug, and the sweet words spoken in innocence. Let me not take for granted these fleeting moments that make up the years. Even in the midst of stress or exhaustion, open my eyes to see the beauty of today. Fill my heart with gratitude for every milestone and memory, and let joy overflow from my soul as I walk this path of motherhood with You. Amen.

Scripture:

"Children are a heritage from the Lord, offspring a reward from him."

– Psalm 127:3

9. Trust in God's Guidance for Their Children

Heavenly God, I want what's best for my children. I want them to grow up happy, healthy, and full of purpose. But I know that I can't control every aspect of their lives or shield them from every challenge. Lord, I need to trust that You are guiding them, that You know their path, and that You have plans to prosper and not harm them. Help me release my fears and anxieties over their future, trusting that Your hand is upon them. Give me wisdom to guide them well, but also Peace to step back and let You work in their lives. Remind me that, ultimately, they are Your children, and You love them more than I ever could. Amen.

Scripture:

"For I know the plans I have for you,' declares the Lord, 'plans to prosper you and not to harm you, plans to give you hope and a future."

— **Jeremiah 29:11**

10. Embracing Imperfection as a Mom

Dear God, I often feel the pressure to be the perfect mom—the mom who never loses her temper, who always knows the right thing to say, and who manages to balance it all seamlessly. But the truth is, I am far from perfect, and some days are just plain hard. Help me to let go of the unrealistic standards I hold myself to. Teach me to embrace my imperfections and show grace to myself when I fall short. Let me remember that it's not about being the perfect mom but about being a loving mom who points her children to You. Let my kids see a mom who isn't afraid to say sorry, who learns from her mistakes, and who loves them fiercely. Remind me that You work through my weaknesses and that Your strength is made perfect in them. Amen.

Scripture:

"The Lord is gracious and compassionate, slow to anger and rich in love."

— **Psalm 145:8**

11. Faith to Overcome Exhaustion and Burnout

Lord, I often find myself running on empty—physically, emotionally, and spiritually. The demands of work, parenting, and life leave me feeling drained and overwhelmed. I know I cannot sustain this pace on my own. I need Your strength to renew my weary heart and soul. Please grant me the faith to believe that You are my source of rest and replenishment. When I am exhausted, help me lean into You, trusting that You will fill me up and carry me through each day. Let your peace replace my anxiety, and let Your joy be my strength even in times of burnout. Amen.

Scripture:

"Come to me, all you who are weary and burdened, and I will give you rest."

— **Matthew 11:28**

12. Prioritizing What Truly Matters

Dear God, in the busyness of my daily life, it's so easy to lose sight of what's truly important. I find myself prioritizing tasks, schedules, and expectations, often at the expense of what really matters—my faith, my family, and my health. Help me to pause, reflect, and realign my priorities with Your will. Give me the discernment to know what needs my immediate attention and what can wait. Teach me to let go of distractions and focus on the things that bring me closer to You and to those I love. May I make choices that honor You and nurture my family and myself. Amen.

Scripture:

"But seek first his kingdom and his righteousness, and all these things will be given to you as well."

— **Matthew 6:33**

13. Confidence in Parenting and Career Choices

Heavenly God, as a mother and a working woman, I often second-guess myself. Did I make the right choice in my career? Am I doing what's best for my family? The weight of these decisions can leave me feeling uncertain and inadequate. But, Lord, I know that You have placed me where I am for a reason. Help me find confidence in the path You've set before me, trusting that You are guiding my steps in both my parenting and my work. Remind me that I don't have to be perfect; I only need to be faithful to the calling You've given me. May I stand firm in my choices and find peace in knowing that You are with me every step of the way. Amen.

Scripture:

"Being confident of this, that he who began a good work in you will carry it on to completion until the day of Christ Jesus."

– Philippians 1:6

14. Clarity in Setting Boundaries

Lord, I struggle with setting boundaries. I often feel torn between the desire to give my all at work and the need to be fully present at home. It's hard to say "no" when others ask for my time and energy, but I know that I can't give my best to anyone without boundaries. Please give me clarity and courage to establish healthy boundaries that honor You and respect my well-being. Help me to communicate these boundaries with love and to see that they are not selfish but necessary for a balanced life. Let me find Peace in knowing that when I set limits, I create more space for what truly matters. Amen.

Scripture:

"Above all else, guard your heart, for everything you do flows from it."

— **Proverbs 4:23**

15. Grace for the Hard Days

God, some days are just hard. Days when nothing seems to go right, when the stress is high, and my patience runs thin. In those moments, I find myself feeling discouraged and defeated. Please give me the grace to handle these tough days with resilience and faith. Let me see the trials as opportunities for growth and refinement. When I fail, help me not to dwell on my shortcomings but to learn from them and move forward. Teach me to extend grace to myself and to others, and let me trust that Your grace is sufficient to carry me through any struggle. Amen.

Scripture:

"But he gives us more grace. That is why Scripture says: 'God opposes the proud but shows favor to the humble.'"

— **James 4:6**

16. Finding Peace in the Middle of Chaos

Lord, my life feels chaotic at times—between work, family, and all the demands on my time, I feel like I'm spinning in circles. Yet, I know that You are the God of Peace, and in You, I can find rest even in the middle of the storm. Help me to surrender my anxieties to You and find a calmness that transcends my circumstances. Let Your Peace fill my heart and mind, helping me to navigate the busyness of life with a sense of purpose and tranquility. Remind me that You are with me in every moment, offering me a peace that the world cannot give. Amen.

Scripture:

"And the Peace of God, which transcends all understanding, will guard your hearts and your minds in Christ Jesus."

– Philippians 4:7

17. Prayer for a Supportive Partner and Teamwork

Dear God, I am grateful for my partner and the support they bring into my life. We both have our own struggles and sometimes, balancing our individual needs and responsibilities can be difficult. Please help us to work together as a team, supporting one another in love, grace, and understanding. Let us communicate openly and encourage each other, especially on the days when life feels overwhelming. Guide us to grow stronger together and lift each other up, creating a home filled with love, respect, and partnership. May we reflect Your love in our teamwork, and may our relationship be a source of joy and strength. Amen.

Scripture:

"Two are better than one, because they have a good return for their labor: If either of them falls down, one can help the other up."

– Ecclesiastes 4:9-10

18. Hope for Dreams and Goals Beyond Motherhood

God, I am grateful for the gift of motherhood and the joy it brings to my life. But there are dreams and goals within me that go beyond my role as a mother—passions and aspirations that I long to pursue.

Help me to see that it's okay to dream and to seek fulfillment in all the areas of my life. Remind me that my identity is not limited to one role and that You have given me gifts and talents to be used for Your glory. Give me the courage to chase after those dreams and to trust that You will provide a way for me to grow, learn, and achieve the desires of my heart. Amen.

Scripture:

"For I know the plans I have for you,' declares the Lord, 'plans to prosper you and not to harm you, plans to give you hope and a future."

– Jeremiah 29:11

19. Love for Ourselves, as well as Our Family

Dear God, it's easy for me to love and care for my family, but often, I find it hard to extend that same love to myself. I am quick to criticize and slow to show myself grace. Help me to see myself as You see me—worthy of love, forgiveness, and care. Let me practice self-compassion, recognizing that I am human and flawed but also deeply loved by You. Teach me to love myself not in a selfish way but in a way that allows me to be a better wife, mother, and friend. Let my love for myself flow from my understanding of Your great love for me. Amen.

Scripture:

"And the second is like it: 'Love your neighbor as yourself.'"

– Matthew 22:39

20. Overcoming Feelings of Being Overwhelmed

Lord, there are moments when I feel completely overwhelmed—by my responsibilities, my worries, and the demands placed on me. In those times, it's easy to feel paralyzed and unsure of where to start. Please help me to pause and take a breath, trusting that I do not have to carry these burdens alone. Let me find rest in You and trust that You will give me the strength to handle each Challenge, one step at a time. Help me to be present, to not be weighed down by what lies ahead, and to remember that You are greater than any problem I face. Amen.

Scripture:

"Cast all your anxiety on him because he cares for you."

— 1 Peter 5:7

21. Trust in God's Timing for Both Career and Family

God, there are seasons when I feel like I'm missing out on career opportunities and other times when I feel like my family needs me more than ever. Balancing these two is never easy, and sometimes, I struggle to know if I'm on the right path. Please help me trust in Your perfect timing for my life—that You know when to open doors and keep them closed. Give me the patience to wait on Your timing and faith to believe that You are working all things for my good. Help me not to rush ahead or lag behind but to walk in step with You, trusting that You will guide both my career and my family in the way they should go. Amen.

Scripture:

"There is a time for everything and a season for every activity under the heavens."

— Ecclesiastes 3:1

22. Joy in Watching Children Grow

Lord, thank You for the privilege of watching my children grow. It is a gift to see them learn, change, and discover who they are becoming. Even when life feels busy and chaotic, help me to pause and take in the precious moments of their childhood—their laughter, their wonder, their milestones. Let me be present to celebrate their growth, support them in their challenges, and cherish the fleeting moments that I know will pass too quickly. Fill my heart with joy and gratitude for the journey of motherhood, and let me never take for granted the blessing of watching my children grow. Amen.

Scripture:

"Children are a heritage from the Lord, offspring a reward from him."

– Psalm 127:3

23. Surrendering Control to God

Dear God, I often try to control every aspect of my life and the lives of my family. I want to protect my children from pain, make sure every decision is perfect, and ensure that everything goes according to plan. But, Lord, I know that I am not in control—You are. Help me to surrender my need for control and to trust that You are working all things for good. Let me release my fears and anxieties to You, knowing that You hold my future and my family's future in Your hands. May I walk in faith, believing that You will provide and guide us every step of the way. Amen.

Scripture:

"Trust in the Lord with all your heart and lean not on your own understanding; in all your ways submit to him, and he will make your paths straight."

— **Proverbs 3:5-6**

24. Unity in Family Decisions

Lord, making decisions as a family is not always easy. Sometimes, we disagree, and it's hard to find a path that works for everyone. Please help us to seek unity in our decisions, to listen to one another with open hearts, and to communicate with love and respect. Let our choices be guided by Your wisdom, and may we be willing to compromise and support one another. Help us to remember that we are on the same team, working together for the good of our family, and let our decisions reflect Your love and purpose for our lives. Amen.

Scripture:

"If a house is divided against itself, that house cannot stand."

— **Mark 3:25**

25. Cultivating Resilience During Busy Seasons

Heavenly God, life feels like a whirlwind right now, with so much to juggle and so little time to catch my breath. In these busy seasons, it's easy to feel discouraged and stretched too thin. But, Lord, I know that You have given me the resilience to face these challenges. Help me to lean on You for strength, to find rest in Your presence, and to press on with hope and determination. Remind me that I am not alone, that

You are my rock and my refuge, and that You will carry me through every storm and season. Amen.

Scripture:

"The Lord is my strength and my shield; my heart trusts in him, and he helps me. My heart leaps for joy, and with my song, I praise him."

– Psalm 28:7

26. Perspective to See Blessings Amidst Challenges

God, sometimes all I see are the challenges—the stressful days, the arguments, the setbacks. It's hard to see beyond the difficulties to recognize the blessings in my life. Help me to change my perspective, to see that even in the midst of struggle, You are at work. Let me find gratitude for the small victories, the growth that comes through hardship, and the love that sustains me through it all. Open my eyes to the blessings that surround me every day, and let my heart overflow with thanksgiving, even in the toughest times. Amen.

Scripture:

"Give thanks in all circumstances, for this is God's will for you in Christ Jesus."

– 1 Thessalonians 5:18

27. Building a Strong Support System

Dear God, I know I am not meant to do life alone. I need community, friendship, and support from those who love me and who share in my journey. Please help me build strong and meaningful connections with others—people who will encourage me, hold me accountable, and walk alongside me in the good times and the struggles. Let me also be a source of support and encouragement to others, building relationships that reflect Your love and grace. Thank You for the people You have placed in my life, and may our relationships be a blessing to one another. Amen.

Scripture:

"Therefore encourage one another and build each other up, just as, in fact, you are doing."

— 1 Thessalonians 5:11

28. Courage to Pursue Career Ambitions

Lord, I have dreams and ambitions that often feel out of reach, and I sometimes fear stepping out into the unknown. Please give me the courage to pursue the passions and goals You have placed in my heart. Let me be bold in seeking opportunities, fearless in trying new things, and confident in the gifts and talents You have given me. Remind me that You are with me wherever I go, guiding my steps and opening doors. Help me to walk in faith, trusting that if You have called me to it, You will equip me for it. Amen.

Scripture:

"Have I not commanded you? Be strong and courageous. Do not be afraid; do not be discouraged, for the Lord your God will be with you wherever you go."

— Joshua 1:9

29. Rest and Sabbath for the Soul

Heavenly God, I am often so busy that I forget to rest—to take time to simply be in Your presence and find renewal for my soul. Help me to honor the Sabbath, to set aside time for rest, reflection, and worship. Let me find Peace in stepping away from my work, knowing that rest is not a sign of weakness but a gift from You. Teach me to trust that You will take care of what I leave 66undone and let my soul find true rest in Your presence. Amen.

Scripture:

"Then he said to them, 'The Sabbath was made for man, not man for the Sabbath.'"

— Mark 2:27

30. Gratitude for the Journey of Balancing Work and Family

Dear Lord, thank You for the beautiful and challenging journey of balancing work and family. It's not always easy, but I am grateful for the opportunities You have given me—to pursue my passions, to provide for my loved ones, and to raise my children in love. Help me to find joy in the journey, even when the road is tough, and to remember that every moment, every Challenge, and every victory is part of a greater purpose. Let me walk this path with a heart full of gratitude, trusting that You are with me every step of the way. Amen.

Scripture:

"And whatever you do, whether in word or deed, do it all in the name of the Lord Jesus, giving thanks to God the God through him."

— Colossians 3:17

Action Steps For Each Prayer:

Let's dive into a simple, meaningful way to incorporate prayer and reflection into your busy day. These action steps are designed with you in mind—quick, heartfelt moments that help you stay connected to God, no matter how hectic life gets.

Interactive 3-Minute Prayer & Reflection Challenge

This is a practical, easy-to-follow practice you can do daily. In just three minutes, you'll reflect, connect with Scripture, and pray in a way that feels personal and impactful. Here's how it works:

Step 1: 1-Minute Reflection Prompt

Start with a simple question that ties the prayer to your day. This moment of reflection helps you pause and notice God's presence. Here are some examples:

- What blessing did I notice today that I can thank God for?

- What challenge can I give to God right now?

Take just one minute to think about your answer and let it guide your heart toward gratitude or surrender.

Step 2: 1-Minute Scripture Focus:

Spend one minute reading and reflecting on a short Scripture verse. Let it resonate with you—repeat it silently in your mind or whisper it as a prayer. Keep it close to your heart throughout the day as a grounding reminder of God's word.

Step 3: 1-Minute Personal Prayer

This is your time to speak to God in your own words. If you need a little structure, try using a customizable template like this:

"Lord, thank You for _____. Please help me with _____. I trust You to guide me in _____."

Personalize it to reflect your current needs and make it authentic to your life.

Daily Gratitude & Praise Prompt

At the end of each day, take a moment to recognize how God was present. Write down one sentence reflecting your gratitude or an experience of His peace. For example:

- *"Today, I felt God's peace when I found strength in a tough moment."*
- *"I'm grateful for God's guidance in making a big decision today."*

This small act of gratitude can help you end the day with a sense of peace and connection.

"Whisper Prayers" for Busy Days

Sometimes, life doesn't allow for long prayers—but that doesn't mean you can't stay connected to God. Whisper prayers are quick, heartfelt one-liners you can say throughout the day. They might look like this:

- "God, give me strength for this meeting."

- "Help me be patient with my kids."

- "Thank You for the sunshine today."

These small prayers are a reminder that God is with you in every moment, no matter how big or small.

These simple steps—reflection, Scripture, personal prayer, gratitude, and whisper prayers—are tools to keep you connected to God throughout your busy days. The 3-Minute Prayer & Reflection Challenge is an easy, manageable way to bring prayer into your routine and grow spiritually, even amidst life's demands. Give it a try, and let it bring you closer to God, one day at a time.

1. Gratitude for the ability to provide for the family

1-Minute Reflection Prompt:

- What is one way God has provided for my family through my work today?

1-Minute Scripture Focus:

- "And God is able to bless you abundantly..." (2 Corinthians 9:8). Reflect on how God has blessed you today.

1-Minute Personal Prayer:

- "God, thank You for providing for my family through ____. Help me find joy in ____ and remind me that my work is a blessing."

Whisper Prayer:

- "Thank You for the roof over our heads."

2. Patience Amidst Hectic Schedules

1-Minute Reflection Prompt:

- Where did I need patience today? How did I respond?

1-Minute Scripture Focus:

- "Be completely humble and gentle; be patient..." (Ephesians 4:2). Ask God to help you show patience tomorrow.

1-Minute Personal Prayer:

- "Lord, today I struggled with patience when ____. Help me to slow down and show love through patience."

Whisper Prayer:

- "Give me patience in this moment."

3. Strength to Face Challenges with Grace

1-Minute Reflection Prompt:

- What challenge am I facing that feels overwhelming? How can I face it with grace?

1-Minute Scripture Focus:

- "My grace is sufficient for you..." (2 Corinthians 12:9). Meditate on God's strength being made perfect in your weakness.

1-Minute Personal Prayer:

- "God, I need Your strength to face ____. Help me to handle it with grace, trusting in Your power."

Whisper Prayer:

- "God, give me strength right now."

4. Wisdom in Making Decisions That Impact the Family

1-Minute Reflection Prompt:

- What decision is weighing heavily on me right now? Have I asked God for wisdom?

1-Minute Scripture Focus:

- "If any of you lacks wisdom, you should ask God..." (James 1:5). Ask God for guidance today.

1-Minute Personal Prayer:

- "Father, I need wisdom for ____. Help me to see what truly matters, and guide me in making the best choice for my family."

Whisper Prayer:

- "God, please guide my decision."

5. Peace in the Present Moment

1-Minute Reflection Prompt:

- What moment of today did I miss because I was too distracted?

1-Minute Scripture Focus:

- "Peace, I leave with you..." (John 14:27). Reflect on how you can invite God's peace into your present moment.

1-Minute Personal Prayer:

- "Lord, help me to be fully present with ____. Give me peace in this moment, knowing You hold tomorrow."

Whisper Prayer:

- "Help me be present, God."

6. Balancing Self-Care and Care for Others

1-Minute Reflection Prompt:

- Did I take any time to care for myself today? How did it impact my mood?

1-Minute Scripture Focus:

- "Your bodies are temples of the Holy Spirit..." (1 Corinthians 6:19). Reflect on how God calls you to care for your body and spirit.

1-Minute Personal Prayer:

- "Father, I often neglect my own needs. Help me to see self-care as a way to serve my family better."

Whisper Prayer:

- "Lord, give me the grace to rest."

7. Letting Go of Guilt for Not "Doing It All"

1-Minute Reflection Prompt:

- What unrealistic expectations did I place on myself today? How can I release it?

1-Minute Scripture Focus:

- "My grace is sufficient for you..." (2 Corinthians 12:9). Ask God to help you embrace your imperfections.

1-Minute Personal Prayer:

- "Lord, I didn't get everything done today, and that's okay. Help me to release my guilt and trust in Your grace."

Whisper Prayer:

- "I am enough with Your grace, God."

8. Joy in the Small Moments of Motherhood

1-Minute Reflection Prompt:

- What small moment with my children brought me joy today?

1-Minute Scripture Focus:

- "Children are a heritage from the Lord..." (Psalm 127:3). Reflect on the gift of your children today.

1-Minute Personal Prayer:

- "Thank You, Lord, for the joy of ____. Help me to cherish these small moments and see the beauty in each day."

Whisper Prayer:

- "Thank You for my children, Lord."

9. Trust in God's Guidance for Their Children

1-Minute Reflection Prompt:

- What concern do I have for my child's future? Have I surrendered it to God?

1-Minute Scripture Focus:

- "For I know the plans I have for you..." (Jeremiah 29:11). Trust God's plans for your children today.

1-Minute Personal Prayer:

- "Lord, I release my worry about ____. I trust that You are guiding them and that Your plans are good."

Whisper Prayer:

- "Guide my children, God."

10. Embracing Imperfection as a mom

1-Minute Reflection Prompt:

- What unrealistic standard did I hold myself to today? How can I show myself grace?

1-Minute Scripture Focus:

- "The Lord is gracious and compassionate..." (Psalm 145:8). Remind yourself that God is gracious, and you can be too.

1-Minute Personal Prayer:

- "God, help me to release my need for perfection. Let me embrace my imperfections and show myself the same grace I show others."

Whisper Prayer:

- "Thank You for Your grace, Lord."

11. Faith to Overcome Exhaustion and Burnout

1-Minute Reflection Prompt:

- Where am I feeling most exhausted today? Have I turned to God for rest?

1-Minute Scripture Focus:

- "Come to me, all you who are weary..." (Matthew 11:28). Ask God for renewal and rest in your spirit.

1-Minute Personal Prayer:

- "God, I am exhausted in ____. I need Your strength and peace to carry me through. Help me rest in You."

Whisper Prayer:

- "Lord, renew my strength today."

12. Prioritizing What Truly Matters

1-Minute Reflection Prompt:

- Did my priorities today reflect what truly matters? What could I realign tomorrow?

1-Minute Scripture Focus:

- "Seek first his kingdom..." (Matthew 6:33). Ask God to help you focus on what is most important.

1-Minute Personal Prayer:

- "God, help me to let go of distractions and focus on what matters most—my relationship with You and my family."

Whisper Prayer:

- "Lord, help me focus on what matters."

13. Confidence in Parenting and Career Choices

1-Minute Reflection Prompt:

- Where do I feel unsure about a decision I made? How can I trust God's plan for me?

1-Minute Scripture Focus:

- "He who began a good work in you..." (Philippians 1:6). Trust that God is guiding your steps in both work and parenting.

1-Minute Personal Prayer:

- "Father, help me trust that I am where You want me to be. Give me peace and confidence in my choices."

Whisper Prayer:

- "God, guide my steps and choices today."

14. Clarity in Setting Boundaries

1-Minute Reflection Prompt:

- Where have I struggled to set a boundary today? How could that boundary bring me peace?

1-Minute Scripture Focus:

- "Guard your heart, for everything you do flows from it..." (Proverbs 4:23). Reflect on how healthy boundaries honor God.

1-Minute Personal Prayer:

- "God, give me the wisdom to set healthy boundaries. Help me to say 'no' when I need to, without guilt."

Whisper Prayer:

- "Lord, give me clarity in setting boundaries."

15. Grace for the Hard Days

1-Minute Reflection Prompt:

- What was the hardest moment today? How can I give myself grace?

1-Minute Scripture Focus:

- "But he gives us more grace..." (James 4:6). Ask God to fill you with grace for yourself and others.

1-Minute Personal Prayer:

- "God, today was difficult, but I know you give me grace. Help me to extend that same grace to myself and others."

Whisper Prayer:

- "Lord, give me grace for today."

16. Finding Peace in the Middle of Chaos

1-Minute Reflection Prompt:

- In what situation today did I feel overwhelmed? How can I invite God's peace into that chaos?

1-Minute Scripture Focus:

- "The peace of God, which transcends all understanding…" (Philippians 4:7). Reflect on God's peace even in the busiest moments.

1-Minute Personal Prayer:

- "Lord, help me find peace in the middle of ____. Remind me that Your peace is always available, even in chaos."

Whisper Prayer:

- "Give me peace in this moment, God."

17. Prayer for a Supportive Partner and Teamwork

1-Minute Reflection Prompt:

- How did my partner or a loved one support me today? How can I express gratitude for them?

1-Minute Scripture Focus:

- "Two are better than one..." (Ecclesiastes 4:9-10). Thank God for the gift of partnership.

1-Minute Personal Prayer:

- "Lord, thank You for ____. Help us to support and encourage one another as we face life together."

Whisper Prayer:

- "God, bless my partner with strength and love."

18. Hope for Dreams and Goals Beyond Motherhood

1-Minute Reflection Prompt:

- What dream has God placed in my heart that I am hesitant to pursue? How can I take a step toward it?

1-Minute Scripture Focus:

- "For I know the plans I have for you..." (Jeremiah 29:11). Reflect on God's plans for you beyond your current role.

1-Minute Personal Prayer:

- "God, I have dreams beyond motherhood. Give me the courage to pursue them and trust that You will make a way."

Whisper Prayer:

- "Help me pursue my dreams, God."

19. Love for Themselves, as Well as Their Family

1-Minute Reflection Prompt:

- What is one way I can show myself love today, just as I show love to my family?

1-Minute Scripture Focus:

- "Love your neighbor as yourself..." (Matthew 22:39). Ask God to help you see yourself as worthy of love and care.

1-Minute Personal Prayer:

- "Lord, help me to show myself the love and care that I show others. Help me see myself as You see me—worthy and loved."

Whisper Prayer:

- "Help me love myself as You love me, God."

20. Overcoming Feelings of Being Overwhelmed

1-Minute Reflection Prompt:

- What's one thing that overwhelmed me today? How can I give that burden to God?

1-Minute Scripture Focus:

- "Cast all your anxiety on him..." (1 Peter 5:7). Reflect on giving your overwhelming feelings to God.

1-Minute Personal Prayer:

- "God, I felt overwhelmed today by ____. I cast that burden on You and trust that You will help me through."

Whisper Prayer:

- "Take my burdens, Lord."

21. Trust in God's Timing for Both Career and Family

1-Minute Reflection Prompt:

- Where am I feeling impatient with the timing in my life? How can I trust God's plan more?

1-Minute Scripture Focus:

"There is a time for everything..." (Ecclesiastes 3:1). Ask God to help you trust His timing in your career and family.

1-Minute Personal Prayer:

- "Lord, I often feel impatient about ____. Help me to trust that Your timing is perfect for both my career and family."

Whisper Prayer:

- "God, help me trust Your timing."

22. Joy in Watching Children Grow

1-Minute Reflection Prompt:

- What growth or milestone did I notice in my child today? How can I celebrate it with gratitude?

1-Minute Scripture Focus:

- "Children are a heritage from the Lord..." (Psalm 127:3). Reflect on the joy of seeing your children grow.

1-Minute Personal Prayer:

- "God, thank You for the gift of watching ____. Help me to celebrate and cherish these moments."

Whisper Prayer:

- "Thank You for my child's growth, Lord."

23. Surrendering Control to God

1-Minute Reflection Prompt:

- What situation am I trying too hard to control? How can I release it to God?

1-Minute Scripture Focus:

- "Trust in the Lord with all your heart..." (Proverbs 3:5-6). Reflect on trusting God to take control.

1-Minute Personal Prayer:

- "Lord, I surrender ____. Help me to trust You with it and stop trying to control everything."

Whisper Prayer:

- "I trust You with this, God."

24. Unity in Family Decisions

1-Minute Reflection Prompt:

- What family decision are we facing that needs God's guidance? How can I invite Him into the discussion?

1-Minute Scripture Focus:

- "If a house is divided..." (Mark 3:25). Pray for unity in your family's decisions.

1-Minute Personal Prayer:

- "God, we need unity in deciding ____. Help us to work together, listen well, and seek Your guidance."

Whisper Prayer:

- "Lord, give us unity in this decision."

25. Cultivating Resilience During Busy Seasons

1-Minute Reflection Prompt:

- What challenge did I overcome today? How can I build resilience through God's strength?

1-Minute Scripture Focus:

- "The Lord is my strength and my shield..." (Psalm 28:7). Reflect on God as your source of resilience.

1-Minute Personal Prayer:

- "Lord, I need Your strength to face ____. Help me to press on, knowing that You are my refuge."

Whisper Prayer:

- "Give me resilience, God."

26. Perspective to See Blessings Amidst Challenges

1-Minute Reflection Prompt:

- What challenge did I face today, and where can I see God's blessing within it?

1-Minute Scripture Focus:

- "Give thanks in all circumstances..." (1 Thessalonians 5:18). Reflect on finding blessings in your challenges.

1-Minute Personal Prayer:

- "God, even in the challenge of ____, I know you are at work. Help me to see and appreciate Your blessings."

27. Building a Strong Support System

1-Minute Reflection Prompt:

- Who in my life has supported me recently? How can I strengthen my relationships with those around me?

1-Minute Scripture Focus:

- "Therefore encourage one another..." (1 Thessalonians 5:11). Reflect on the gift of community and encouragement.

1-Minute Personal Prayer:

- "Lord, thank You for the people You've placed in my life. Help me to be a source of support and encouragement to those around me."

Whisper Prayer:

- "God, strengthen my support system."

28. Courage to Pursue Career Ambitions

1-Minute Reflection Prompt:

- What dream or goal have I been hesitant to pursue? How can I take a small step toward it today?

1-Minute Scripture Focus:

- "Be strong and courageous…" (Joshua 1:9). Ask God for the courage to pursue the dreams He has placed in your heart.

1-Minute Personal Prayer:

- "God, I feel unsure about pursuing ____. Give me the courage to take the first step, trusting You to guide me."

Whisper Prayer:

- "Lord, give me courage for this dream."

29. Rest and Sabbath for the Soul

1-Minute Reflection Prompt:

- Have I taken any time to rest today? How can I prioritize rest as an act of worship?

1-Minute Scripture Focus:

- "The Sabbath was made for man…" (Mark 2:27). Reflect on the importance of rest for your spiritual and physical health.

1-Minute Personal Prayer:

- "Lord, help me to find rest for my soul in You. Teach me to step away from busyness and find peace in Your presence."

Whisper Prayer:

- "God, help me rest today."

30. Gratitude for the Journey of Balancing Work and Family

1-Minute Reflection Prompt:

- How have I seen God's hand in balancing work and family today? What am I most grateful for?

1-Minute Scripture Focus:

- "And whatever you do, whether in word or deed..." (Colossians 3:17). Reflect on how God gives purpose and strength in your daily balancing act.

1-Minute Personal Prayer:

- "God, thank You for helping me balance work and family. Help me to find joy and gratitude in this journey, trusting You every step of the way."

Whisper Prayer:

- "Thank You for guiding me, Lord."

Chapter Two:
Leading with Grace: Prayers for Women in Leadership and Life

This chapter is crafted for those of us who are in leadership positions. Each prayer is designed to guide and support us leaders through various leadership challenges, providing spiritual strength and clarity when needed.

The prayer for strength to lead with integrity helps us stay true to our values, even when taking the easier path feels tempting. It serves as a reminder that integrity is the cornerstone of authentic leadership.

When faced with tough decisions, the prayer for knowledge equips us to make wise choices for ourselves and those who depend on our guidance. It encourages thoughtful, informed leadership rooted in service.

For those moments when standing firm in our beliefs feels daunting, the prayer for boldness offers courage and resilience. It strengthens our resolve to lead with conviction, even in opposition.

To ground our leadership in humility, the prayer for a humble heart reminds us that authentic leadership is about serving others, not wielding power. It helps us focus on lifting others while staying connected to our purpose.

The prayer for confidence supports us in moments of self-doubt, reminding us of our divine calling and purpose. It empowers us to step into our roles with faith and assurance, inspiring confidence in those we lead.

The prayer for faith encourages us to be role models for our teams, fostering an environment where growth and inspiration flourish. It helps us align our actions with our values, setting an example for others to follow.

Finally, the prayer for patience is our anchor in challenging moments. It equips us to respond to difficult situations with kindness, leading with a steady heart and a clear mind.

Each of these prayers is a tool to help us navigate the complexities of leadership, ensuring that we can lead with integrity, wisdom, and grace. This chapter is our spiritual resource, tailored to meet the diverse demands of our leadership journey.

1. Strength for Leading with Integrity

Heavenly God, thank You for placing me in a leadership role. I know that with leadership comes responsibility, and I desire to lead with integrity. When it's tempting to take shortcuts, compromise values for success, or lead in a way that doesn't honor You, please give me the strength to choose integrity. Let my words match my actions, and let my decisions reflect honesty and fairness.

Help me inspire others to lead with integrity as well, and may my leadership reflect Your character. Amen.

Scripture:

"The integrity of the upright guides them, but the unfaithful are destroyed by their duplicity."

– Proverbs 11:3

2. Wisdom in Decision-Making

Dear Lord, every day brings new decisions—some small, some significant—that impact my team and the people I lead. I don't always know the right path, and I can easily feel overwhelmed by the weight of my choices. Please grant me the wisdom to make decisions that honor You and serve the greater good. Let Your guidance be my compass, and may I seek counsel when needed. Help me to weigh each decision carefully, with discernment and understanding. Let my choices bring about growth, unity, and success for those I lead. Amen.

Scripture:

"If any of you lacks wisdom, you should ask God, who gives generously to all without finding fault, and it will be given to you."

– James 1:5

3. Courage to Stand Firm in Values

Lord, leadership often requires standing firm in values and principles, even when it's not popular or easy. When faced with opposition or pressure to compromise, it help me to be courageous. Give me the boldness to speak the truth, to uphold what is right, and to act in a way that honors You. Let me be unwavering in my commitment to ethical and moral leadership. And when the world around me says to bend, let me stand strong, knowing that You are my source of strength and courage. Amen.

Scripture:

"Be on your guard; stand firm in the faith; be courageous; be strong."

– 1 Corinthians 16:13

4. Humility in Leadership Roles

God, as a leader, it is easy to become prideful or to see leadership as a position of power. But I know that true leadership is about service, humility, and putting others first. Help me to lead with a humble heart, recognizing that every success is a result of Your grace and the efforts of my team. Let me be quick to listen, slow to speak, and willing to learn from those I lead. May I always approach my role as an opportunity to serve, uplift, and honor those around me. Amen.

Scripture:

"Humble yourselves before the Lord, and he will lift you up."

– James 4:10

5. Confidence to Step into Authority

Lord, sometimes I doubt my ability to lead. I question whether I have what it takes or fear that I am not enough. But I know that You have called me to this position for a reason. Please help me find confidence in Your calling, knowing that You have equipped me with the gifts, skills, and wisdom I need. Let me walk in authority—not with arrogance, but with assurance that You are working through me. Help me to lead boldly and faithfully, trusting in Your strength and guidance. Amen.

Scripture:

"So do not throw away your confidence; it will be richly rewarded."

— **Hebrews 10:35**

6. Faith to Inspire and Influence Others Positively

Dear God, I desire to be a leader who inspires others to grow, to be better, and to reach their fullest potential. Let my faith be a light to those I lead, and may my actions and words bring encouragement and positivity. Help me to lead with a servant's heart, to lift up those who are struggling, and to create a culture of support and empowerment. May my leadership be a testament to Your love, grace, and hope. Use me to make a positive impact in the lives of those I influence. Amen.

Scripture:

"In the same way, let your light shine before others, that they may see your good deeds and glorify your God in heaven."

— **Matthew 5:16**

7. Patience in Difficult Situations

Lord, leadership comes with its challenges—moments of conflict, setbacks, and difficult decisions. There are times when my patience is tested, and I feel frustrated or disheartened. Please grant me patience to handle these situations with grace and wisdom. Help me to respond calmly, to listen without judgment, and to approach every Challenge as an opportunity for growth. Let me be a calming presence for my team and lead with a steady heart, trusting that You are working even in the midst of difficulty. Amen.

Scripture:

"Be completely humble and gentle; be patient, bearing with one another in love."

— **Ephesians 4:2**

8. Gratitude for Leadership Opportunities

Heavenly God, thank You for placing me in a position of leadership. It is a privilege to be able to serve others and to help guide a team toward a shared goal. When I feel overwhelmed or discouraged, remind me of the blessing it is to lead. Help me to see each day as an opportunity to grow, learn, and make a difference. Let gratitude fill my heart, and may I always remember that leadership is not about power but about service and stewardship of the opportunities You have provided. Amen.

Scripture:

"And whatever you do, whether in word or deed, do it all in the name of the Lord Jesus, giving thanks to God the God through him."

— **Colossians 3:17**

9. Vision to Lead Teams Effectively

God, as a leader, I need to have a clear vision for my team—to know where we are going and how to get there. Please grant me the vision to lead effectively, set meaningful and achievable goals, and inspire my team to work toward a common purpose. Help me communicate that vision with clarity and passion, and may we work together in unity toward success. Let Your wisdom guide every step we take, and may our efforts reflect Your glory. Amen.

Scripture:

"Where there is no vision, the people perish: but he that keepeth the law, happy is he."

– Proverbs 29:18 (KJV)

10. Resilience to Face Challenges with Grace

Lord, leadership is not without its struggles, and there are days when I face setbacks, disappointments, and obstacles that seem impossible to overcome. Please give me the resilience to face these challenges with grace, to rise above adversity, and to keep pushing forward with faith. Let me see challenges as opportunities for growth and help me to remain hopeful even in difficult times. May my resilience be a testimony to Your strength and a source of encouragement to those around me. Amen.

Scripture:

"Not only so, but we also glory in our sufferings because we know that suffering produces perseverance; perseverance, character; and character, hope."

– Romans 5:3-4

11. Compassion for Team Members and Peers

Dear God, help me to be a leader who leads with compassion and understanding. Let me see my team members as individuals with their own struggles, hopes, and dreams. Help me to be patient when they make mistakes, encouraging when they are discouraged, and a listening ear when they need support. Let my leadership be rooted in love and empathy, and may I create a safe and supportive environment where each person feels valued and heard. Amen.

Scripture:

"Finally, all of you, be like-minded, be sympathetic, love one another, be compassionate and humble."

— 1 Peter 3:8

12. Encouragement in the Face of Doubts

God, there are times when I doubt my ability to lead—when I question whether I am equipped, whether I am making the right decisions, or whether I am truly making a difference. In those moments of doubt, please fill me with encouragement and remind me of the gifts and abilities You have given me. Help me to trust that You are guiding my path and that I am never alone in this journey. Let me find confidence not in my own strength but in Yours, knowing that You are using me for a greater purpose. Amen.

Scripture:

"But now, this is what the Lord says... 'Do not fear, for I have redeemed you; I have summoned you by name; you are mine.'"

— Isaiah 43:1

13. Trust in God's Leadership Over Their Life

Dear Lord, as I lead others, help me to always remember that You are the ultimate leader of my life. Let me submit to Your guidance and trust in Your plan, knowing that You see the bigger picture. When I am uncertain or feel lost, remind me that You are directing my steps and that I can lean on You for wisdom, strength, and direction. Help me to surrender my ambitions, fears, and decisions to You, and let me lead others as You lead me—with love, humility, and purpose. Amen.

Scripture:

"Trust in the Lord with all your heart and lean not on your own understanding; in all your ways submit to him, and he will make your paths straight."

– Proverbs 3:5-6

14. Peace Amidst Stressful Responsibilities

Lord, leadership often comes with stress and heavy responsibilities. There are days when I feel overwhelmed by the pressure to perform, to meet deadlines, and to navigate complex situations. Please give me Your Peace—a peace that surpasses all understanding—to calm my heart and mind. Help me to approach my responsibilities with confidence and a sense of calm, knowing that You are with me. Let Your Peace fill me so that I may lead others with a steady heart and a clear mind. Amen.

Scripture:

"Peace I leave with you; my Peace I give you. I do not give to you as the world gives. Do not let your hearts be troubled, and do not be afraid."

– John 14:27

15. Grace When Handling Conflicts

Dear God, conflicts are inevitable in leadership, and there are times when disagreements arise and tempers flare. Help me to approach these moments with grace and wisdom. Let me listen openly, respond with kindness, and seek resolution rather than division. May I be quick to forgive and slow to anger, and may my actions reflect Your love and Peace. Help me to handle conflicts in a way that honors You and brings healing and unity to those involved. Amen.

Scripture:

"A gentle answer turns away wrath, but a harsh word stirs up anger."

– Proverbs 15:1

16. Clarity of Purpose in Leadership

God, help me understand and embrace the purpose for which You have called me to lead. Let me not be distracted by others' opinions or the pressures of the world but instead, stay focused on the calling and vision You have given me. Guide my decisions, actions, and interactions with clarity and intentionality. May my leadership be driven by a desire to serve others and to bring glory to You. Amen.

Scripture:

"Commit to the Lord whatever you do, and he will establish your plans."

– Proverbs 16:3

17. Motivation to Continue Growing as a Leader

Dear God, I know that leadership is a journey of growth, learning, and continuous improvement. Help me to stay motivated to grow as a leader, to seek out opportunities for development, and to learn from my experiences. Let me be open to feedback, willing to try new things, and eager to grow in my skills and understanding. May I never become complacent but always strive to be a better leader for those I serve. Amen.

Scripture:

"The wise store up knowledge, but the mouth of a fool invites ruin."

– Proverbs 10:14

18. Balance Between Work and Personal Life

Lord, being a leader can sometimes mean sacrificing time and energy for the sake of the job. But I know that You desire balance and wholeness for me. Help me to find a healthy balance between my work and my personal life so that I can be fully present with my loved ones and take care of my own well-being. Let me remember that leadership does not mean overworking or neglecting myself but serving from a place of health and wholeness. Amen.

Scripture:

"The Lord gives strength to his people; the Lord blesses his people with peace."

– Psalm 29:11

19. Perseverance to Lead in Difficult Times

God, there will be times when leadership is tough—when progress is slow, when obstacles seem insurmountable, and when I feel like giving up. Please grant me the perseverance to press on in these moments, to keep my eyes on the vision, and to lead with faith and determination. Let me not grow weary in doing good, but continue to trust that You are working through every Challenge. Help me be a leader who perseveres, encourages others to keep going, and remains faithful in the good times and the hard times. Amen.

Scripture:

"Let us not become weary in doing good, for at the proper time, we will reap a harvest if we do not give up."

– Galatians 6:9

20. Joy in Seeing Team Successes

Lord, thank You for the joy of leading a team and seeing their hard work pay off. It is a blessing to watch them grow, succeed, and achieve great things together. Help me to celebrate their victories, to lift them up in their accomplishments, and to share in their joy. Let my leadership bring out the best in those I serve, and may we all find joy in working together for a common goal. Amen.

Scripture:

"Rejoice with those who rejoice; mourn with those who mourn."

– Romans 12:15

21. Seeking God's Guidance in Leadership Roles

Dear God, I want to be a leader who seeks Your guidance in every decision, action, and interaction. Help me to seek You first, pray for wisdom, and trust in Your direction for my leadership. Let me be sensitive to Your Spirit's leading, and may my decisions reflect Your heart and Your will. Guide my steps, Lord, and help me to lead others in a way that honors You. Amen.

Scripture:

"Your word is a lamp for my feet, a light on my path."

— Psalm 119:105

22. Restoring Energy and Strength Regularly

God, leadership can be draining, and sometimes, I feel depleted in energy and strength. Please help me to find ways to rest, recharge, and renew my spirit. Let me not feel guilty for taking time to step away and care for myself. May I find rest in You and let Your presence fill me with the energy and strength I need to lead well. Amen.

Scripture:

"He gives strength to the weary and increases the power of the weak."

— Isaiah 40:29

23. Trusting the Process of Leadership Growth

Lord, growth as a leader is a journey, and sometimes, I want to rush the process or skip over the lessons You are teaching me. Help me to trust that every experience, Challenge, and victory is shaping me into the leader You have called me to be. Let me be patient with myself, knowing that growth takes time, and help me to learn and grow from every step of the journey. Amen.

Scripture:

"Being confident of this, that he who began a good work in you will carry it on to completion until the day of Christ Jesus."

— Philippians 1:6

24. Empathy in Understanding Team Needs

Dear God, as a leader, I want to understand my team members' needs, hopes, and struggles. Help me be empathetic, listen with compassion, and respond with care. Let me see each person as valuable and unique, and may my leadership reflect a heart that cares deeply for those I serve. Help me build trust and create an environment where each person feels understood and supported. Amen.

Scripture:

"Rejoice with those who rejoice; mourn with those who mourn."

— Romans 12:15

25. Adaptability to Change and New Challenges

God, the world constantly changes, and leadership requires adaptability and flexibility. When new challenges arise, they help me to be open to change, willing to learn, and ready to adjust my plans. Let me approach every change with a positive attitude and a willingness to grow. May I be a leader who embraces the unknown, knowing that You are with me in every new Challenge and every season of change. Amen.

Scripture:

"For I know the plans I have for you,' declares the Lord, 'plans to prosper you and not to harm you, plans to give you hope and a future."

– **Jeremiah 29:11**

26. Support for Fellow Female Leaders

Dear Lord, As a woman in leadership, I know the value of having support and encouragement from other women who share in this journey. Help me to be a source of support for my fellow female leaders—to lift them up, encourage them in their dreams, and stand with them in their struggles. Let us be a community that empowers one another and builds each other up. May we work together to create a culture of unity, respect, and strength. Amen.

Scripture:

"Therefore encourage one another and build each other up, just as, in fact, you are doing."

– **1 Thessalonians 5:11**

27. Fostering a Culture of Inclusivity and Respect

Lord, help me to create a culture within my team that values inclusivity, respect, and diversity. Let every person feel valued, heard, and respected for who they are and what they bring to the table. Teach me to lead in a way that celebrates differences, encourages open dialogue, and fosters a sense of belonging for all. May my leadership create an environment where everyone feels welcome and supported. Amen.

Scripture:

"Do to others as you would have them do to you."

– Luke 6:31

28. Prayer for Those They Lead and Influence

Dear God, I lift up my team to You—the people I lead, work alongside, and influence. Please bless each person with wisdom, strength, and guidance in their work and in their lives. Help me to be a leader who encourages them, supports their growth, and cares for their well-being. Let my influence be one of positivity, hope, and encouragement, and may my leadership be a blessing to those around me. Amen.

Scripture:

"I always thank my God for you because of his grace given you in Christ Jesus."

– 1 Corinthians 1:4

29. Overcoming Fear of Making Mistakes

God, leadership comes with the fear of making mistakes, of failing, and of letting others down. Please help me to overcome this fear and to lead with boldness and confidence. Let me see mistakes not as failures but as opportunities to learn and grow. Remind me that Your grace covers my imperfections

30. Gratitude for the Opportunity to Lead and Make an Impact

Heavenly God, thank You for entrusting me with the opportunity to lead and influence others. I recognize that this role is not just a position but a privilege—a chance to make a difference in the lives of my team, clients, and community. Help me to approach every day with a heart full of gratitude for the chance to inspire, guide, and impact those around me. Let me never take for granted the platform You have given me, and may my leadership be marked by service, humility, and a desire to reflect Your love in all that I do. Help me to lead with a clear vision, an open heart, and a willingness to make a positive difference in the world. Amen.

*Scripture:

"For we are God's handiwork, created in Christ Jesus to do good works, which God prepared in advance for us to do."

– Ephesians 2:10*

Action Steps For Each Prayer:

1. Strength for Leading with Integrity

1-Minute Reflection Prompt:

- "What situation today might require me to lead with integrity?"

1-Minute Scripture Focus:

- "The integrity of the upright guides them, but the unfaithful are destroyed by their duplicity." — Proverbs 11:3

1-Minute Personal Prayer:

- "God, today I trust You with my actions and decisions. I'm grateful for the strength You provide. Please help me act with honesty and integrity."

Daily Gratitude & Praise Prompt:

- "Today, I felt God's guidance in a decision when ____."

Whisper Prayers:

- "Lord, help me stay true to my values in this moment."

2. Wisdom in Decision-Making

1-Minute Reflection Prompt:

- "What decision do I need wisdom for today?"

1-Minute Scripture Focus:

- "If any of you lacks wisdom, let him ask of God, who gives to all liberally and without reproach." — James 1:5

1-Minute Personal Prayer:

- "God, I trust You with the decisions I face today. I'm grateful for Your wisdom. Please guide my thoughts and choices."

Daily Gratitude & Praise Prompt:

- "Today, I felt God's wisdom when ____."

Whisper Prayers:

- "Lord, give me clarity and discernment right now."

3. Courage to Stand Firm in Values

1-Minute Reflection Prompt:

- "In what situation might I need the courage to uphold my values today?"

1-Minute Scripture Focus:

- "Be strong and courageous. Do not be afraid; do not be discouraged, for the Lord your God will be with you." — Joshua 1:9

1-Minute Personal Prayer:

- "God, I trust You with my fears. I'm grateful for Your presence. Give me the courage to stand firm in my values."

Daily Gratitude & Praise Prompt:

- "Today, I felt God's courage when ____."

Whisper Prayers:

- "God, strengthen me to stay true to my beliefs."

4. Humility in Leadership Roles

1-Minute Reflection Prompt:

- "How can I show humility in my interactions today?"

1-Minute Scripture Focus:

- "Do nothing out of selfish ambition or vain conceit. Rather, in humility value others above yourselves." — Philippians 2:3

1-Minute Personal Prayer:

- "God, I trust You to lead through me. I'm grateful for my role. Help me lead with humility and kindness."

Daily Gratitude & Praise Prompt:

- "Today, I felt God's presence in my humility when____."

Whisper Prayers:

- "Lord, keep my heart humble in this moment."

5. Confidence to Step into Authority

1-Minute Reflection Prompt:

- "What opportunity today requires me to step confidently into my role?"

1-Minute Scripture Focus:

- "For the Spirit God gave us does not make us timid, but gives us power, love, and self-discipline." — 2 Timothy 1:7

1-Minute Personal Prayer:

- "God, I trust You with my role. I'm grateful for the confidence You give me. Help me lead boldly."

Daily Gratitude & Praise Prompt:

- "Today, I felt God's confidence when ____."

Whisper Prayers:

- "Lord, give me boldness in this meeting."

6. Faith to Inspire and Influence Others Positively

1-Minute Reflection Prompt:

- "How can my faith positively influence others today?"

1-Minute Scripture Focus:

- "Let your light shine before others, that they may see your good deeds and glorify your God in heaven." — Matthew 5:16

1-Minute Personal Prayer:

- "God, I trust You with my influence. I'm grateful for Your light. Help me inspire others with faith."

Daily Gratitude & Praise Prompt:

- "Today, I felt God's influence through me when____."

Whisper Prayers:

- "Lord, let Your light shine through me."

7. Patience in Difficult Situations

1-Minute Reflection Prompt:

- "What situation today requires extra patience?"

1-Minute Scripture Focus:

- "Be completely humble and gentle; be patient, bearing with one another in love." — Ephesians 4:2

1-Minute Personal Prayer:

- "God, I trust You with my frustrations. I'm grateful for Your patience with me. Help me show patience to others."

Daily Gratitude & Praise Prompt:

- "Today, I felt God's patience when ____."

Whisper Prayers:

- "Lord, grant me patience in this moment."

8. Gratitude for Leadership Opportunities

1-Minute Reflection Prompt:

- "What aspect of my role am I grateful for today?"

1-Minute Scripture Focus:

- "Give thanks in all circumstances, for this is God's will for you in Christ Jesus." — 1 Thessalonians 5:18

1-Minute Personal Prayer:

- "God, I trust You with my journey. I'm grateful for this opportunity to lead. Help me serve with a grateful heart."

Daily Gratitude & Praise Prompt:

- "Today, I thanked God for ____ in my leadership role."

Whisper Prayers:

- "Thank You, Lord, for this chance to lead."

9. Vision to Lead Teams Effectively

1-Minute Reflection Prompt:

- "How can I help my team stay focused on our shared vision today?"

1-Minute Scripture Focus:

- "Where there is no vision, the people perish." — Proverbs 29:18

1-Minute Personal Prayer:

- "God, I trust You with our goals. I'm grateful for Your guidance. Help me lead with clarity and vision."

Daily Gratitude & Praise Prompt:

- "Today, I felt God's vision for our team when ____."

Whisper Prayers:

- "Lord, guide my steps in leading this team."

10. Resilience to Face Challenges with Grace

1-Minute Reflection Prompt:

- "What challenge today can I face with resilience and grace?"

1-Minute Scripture Focus:

- "But the one who stands firm to the end will be saved." — Matthew 24:13

1-Minute Personal Prayer:

- "God, I trust You with my struggles. I'm grateful for Your strength. Help me face challenges with grace."

Daily Gratitude & Praise Prompt:

- "Today, I felt God's resilience within me when ____."

Whisper Prayers:

- "Lord, strengthen me to handle this with grace."

11. Compassion for Team Members and Peers

1-Minute Reflection Prompt:

- "How can I show compassion to my team or a colleague today?"

1-Minute Scripture Focus:

- "Be kind and compassionate to one another, forgiving each other, just as in Christ God forgave you." — Ephesians 4:32

1-Minute Personal Prayer:

- "God, I trust You to guide my heart. I'm grateful for the people I work with. Help me show compassion and understanding."

Daily Gratitude & Praise Prompt:

- "Today, I felt God's compassion when I _____."

Whisper Prayers:

- "Lord, give me a compassionate heart today."

12. Encouragement in the Face of Doubts

1-Minute Reflection Prompt:

- "What doubts am I holding onto that I need encouragement for?"

1-Minute Scripture Focus:

- "But encourage one another daily, as long as it is called 'Today.'" — Hebrews 3:13

1-Minute Personal Prayer:

- "God, I trust You with my uncertainties. I'm grateful for Your encouragement. Strengthen my heart in moments of doubt."

Daily Gratitude & Praise Prompt:

"Today, I felt God's encouragement when _____."

Whisper Prayers:

- "Lord, help me to stay encouraged despite my doubts."

13. Trust in God's Leadership Over Their Life

1-Minute Reflection Prompt:

- "Where do I need to release control and trust God's leadership?"

1-Minute Scripture Focus:

- "Trust in the Lord with all your heart and lean not on your own understanding." — Proverbs 3:5

1-Minute Personal Prayer:

- "God, I trust You with my journey. I'm grateful for Your guidance. Lead me in every step I take."

Daily Gratitude & Praise Prompt:

- "Today, I trusted God with ____."

Whisper Prayers:

- "Lord, lead me in Your wisdom."

14. Peace Amidst Stressful Responsibilities

1-Minute Reflection Prompt:

- "Where do I need peace amidst today's responsibilities?"

1-Minute Scripture Focus:

- "Peace I leave with you; my peace I give you." — John 14:27

1-Minute Personal Prayer:

- "God, I trust You with my stress. I'm grateful for Your peace. Calm my heart as I face today's responsibilities."

Daily Gratitude & Praise Prompt:

- "Today, I felt God's peace when ____."

Whisper Prayers:

- "Lord, bring me peace in this moment."

15. Grace When Handling Conflicts

1-Minute Reflection Prompt:

- "How can I approach conflict with grace today?"

1-Minute Scripture Focus:

- "Let your conversation be always full of grace, seasoned with salt." — Colossians 4:6

1-Minute Personal Prayer:

- "God, I trust You to guide my words. I'm grateful for Your grace. Help me handle conflict with patience and kindness."

Daily Gratitude & Praise Prompt:

- "Today, I showed grace in conflict when ____."

Whisper Prayers:

- "Lord, give me grace in this conversation."

16. Clarity of Purpose in Leadership

1-Minute Reflection Prompt:

- "What is my purpose in today's responsibilities?"

1-Minute Scripture Focus:

- "Commit to the Lord whatever you do, and He will establish your plans." — Proverbs 16:3

1-Minute Personal Prayer:

- "God, I trust You with my purpose. I'm grateful for the path You set before me. Help me lead with clear intentions."

Daily Gratitude & Praise Prompt:

- "Today, I felt clarity of purpose when ____."

Whisper Prayers:

- "Lord, focus my heart on my purpose."

17. Motivation to Continue Growing as a Leader

1-Minute Reflection Prompt:

- "What can I do today to grow as a leader?"

1-Minute Scripture Focus:

- "Let us not become weary in doing good, for at the proper time we will reap a harvest if we do not give up." — Galatians 6:9

1-Minute Personal Prayer:

- "God, I trust You with my growth. I'm grateful for each learning opportunity. Help me stay motivated to keep improving."

Daily Gratitude & Praise Prompt:

- "Today, I took a step in my growth as a leader when____."

Whisper Prayers:

- "Lord, strengthen my drive to grow."

18. Balance Between Work and Personal Life

1-Minute Reflection Prompt:

- "How can I create balance in my day today?"

1-Minute Scripture Focus:

- "There is a time for everything, and a season for every activity under the heavens." — Ecclesiastes 3:1

1-Minute Personal Prayer:

- "God, I trust You with my time. I'm grateful for each moment. Help me find balance between work and personal life."

Daily Gratitude & Praise Prompt:

- "Today, I felt balanced when ____."

Whisper Prayers:

- "Lord, guide me to balance my responsibilities."

19. Perseverance to Lead in Difficult Times

1-Minute Reflection Prompt:

- "What challenge requires my perseverance today?"

1-Minute Scripture Focus:

- "Blessed is the one who perseveres under trial." — James 1:12

1-Minute Personal Prayer:

- "God, I trust You with my challenges. I'm grateful for Your strength. Help me persevere through difficult times."

Daily Gratitude & Praise Prompt:

- "Today, I showed perseverance when ____."

Whisper Prayers:

- "Lord, give me strength to push forward."

20. Joy in Seeing Team Successes

1-Minute Reflection Prompt:

- "How can I celebrate my team's successes today?"

1-Minute Scripture Focus:

- "Rejoice with those who rejoice." — Romans 12:15

1-Minute Personal Prayer:

- "God, I trust You with our accomplishments. I'm grateful for my team. Help me find joy in their successes."

Daily Gratitude & Praise Prompt:

- "Today, I celebrated my team's success when ____."

Whisper Prayers:

- "Thank You, Lord, for my team's hard work."

21. Seeking God's Guidance in Leadership Roles

1-Minute Reflection Prompt:

- "What decision requires God's guidance today?"

1-Minute Scripture Focus:

- "Show me your ways, Lord, teach me your paths." — Psalm 25:4

1-Minute Personal Prayer:

- "God, I trust You to lead me. I'm grateful for Your wisdom. Guide me in each choice I make."

Daily Gratitude & Praise Prompt:

- "Today, I sought God's guidance when ____."

Whisper Prayers:

- "Lord, direct my steps."

22. Restoring Energy and Strength Regularly

1-Minute Reflection Prompt:

- "What small step can I take today to restore my energy?"

1-Minute Scripture Focus:

- "Come to me, all you who are weary and burdened, and I will give you rest." — Matthew 11:28

1-Minute Personal Prayer:

- "God, I trust You with my rest. I'm grateful for moments to recharge. Help me find renewal in You."

Daily Gratitude & Praise Prompt:

- "Today, I felt restored when ____."

Whisper Prayers:

- "Lord, renew my energy today."

23. Trusting the Process of Leadership Growth

1-Minute Reflection Prompt:

- "How can I embrace the growth process today?"

1-Minute Scripture Focus:

- "Being confident of this, that He who began a good work in you will carry it on to completion." — Philippians 1:6

1-Minute Personal Prayer:

- "God, I trust You with my growth. I'm grateful for Your guidance. Help me be patient with the process."

Daily Gratitude & Praise Prompt:

- "Today, I embraced my growth process by _____."

Whisper Prayers:

- "Lord, help me trust in my journey."

24. Empathy in Understanding Team Needs

1-Minute Reflection Prompt:

- "How can I show empathy to a team member today?"

1-Minute Scripture Focus:

- "Rejoice with those who rejoice; mourn with those who mourn." — Romans 12:15

1-Minute Personal Prayer:

- "God, I trust You with my team's needs. I'm grateful for the empathy You instilled in me. Help me to understand and support my team."

Daily Gratitude & Praise Prompt:

- "Today, I felt God's empathy when _____."

Whisper Prayers:

- "Lord, help me be compassionate today."

25. Adaptability to Change and New Challenges

1-Minute Reflection Prompt:

- "What change today requires my adaptability?"

1-Minute Scripture Focus:

- "For I know the plans I have for you, declares the Lord." — Jeremiah 29:11

1-Minute Personal Prayer:

- "God, I trust You with every change. I'm grateful for Your guidance. Help me adapt to new challenges."

Daily Gratitude & Praise Prompt:

- "Today, I adapted to change by ____."

Whisper Prayers:

- "Lord, give me flexibility for what lies ahead."

26. Support for Fellow Female Leaders

1-Minute Reflection Prompt:

- "How can I support another female leader today?"

1-Minute Scripture Focus:

- "Therefore, encourage one another and build each other up." — 1 Thessalonians 5:11

1-Minute Personal Prayer:

- "God, I trust You to build up leaders. I'm grateful for the women around me. Help me support and encourage them."

Daily Gratitude & Praise Prompt:

- "Today, I supported a fellow leader by ____."

Whisper Prayers:

- "Lord, help me uplift those around me."

27. Fostering a Culture of Inclusivity and Respect

1-Minute Reflection Prompt:

- "What can I do to make my team feel included today?"

1-Minute Scripture Focus:

- "There is neither Jew nor Gentile, slave nor free, male nor female, for you are all one in Christ Jesus." — Galatians 3:28

1-Minute Personal Prayer:

- "God, I trust You with my team's unity. I'm grateful for diversity. Help me foster inclusivity and respect."

Daily Gratitude & Praise Prompt:

- "Today, I promoted inclusivity when ____."

Whisper Prayers:

- "Lord, help me create a welcoming environment."

28. Prayer for Those They Lead and Influence

1-Minute Reflection Prompt:

- "Who can I lift up in prayer today from my team?"

1-Minute Scripture Focus:

- "I urge, then, first of all, that petitions, prayers, intercession, and thanksgiving be made for all people." — 1 Timothy 2:1

1-Minute Personal Prayer:

- "God, I trust You with each person I lead. I'm grateful for the chance to influence them. Bless and guide them today."

Daily Gratitude & Praise Prompt:

- "Today, I prayed for ____ in my leadership."

Whisper Prayers:

- "Lord, guide those I lead."

29. Overcoming Fear of Making Mistakes

1-Minute Reflection Prompt:

- "What fear can I release to God today?"

1-Minute Scripture Focus:

- "There is no fear in love. But perfect love drives out fear." — 1 John 4:18

1-Minute Personal Prayer:

- "God, I trust You with my uncertainties. I'm grateful for Your perfect love. Help me overcome my fear of mistakes."

Daily Gratitude & Praise Prompt:

- "Today, I released fear when ____."

Whisper Prayers:

- "Lord, take away my fears."

30. Gratitude for the Opportunity to Lead and Make an Impact

1-Minute Reflection Prompt:

- "How have I made a positive impact today?"

1-Minute Scripture Focus:

- "And whatever you do, whether in word or deed, do it all in the name of the Lord Jesus." — Colossians 3:17

1-Minute Personal Prayer:

- "God, I trust You with my influence. I'm grateful for the chance to lead. Help me to use this role to make a positive impact."

Daily Gratitude & Praise Prompt:

- "Today, I felt grateful for my role when ____."

Whisper Prayers:

- "Thank You, Lord, for the opportunity to lead."

Chapter Three:
Building Dreams: Prayers for Entrepreneurs and Creative Visionaries

As entrepreneurs and business owners, you deal with unique challenges every day—challenges that need clarity, strength, and guidance. These prayers are meant to give you that spiritual support, bringing you peace, inspiration, and the strength you need as you proceed on your journey. If you're dealing with uncertainty, trying to find wisdom for those tough choices, or just needing a bit of patience while things move slowly, these prayers really connect with the challenges you're facing.

Every prayer is designed just for you, whether you're looking to align your business vision with your purpose, find the courage to take some risks, or keep your feet on the ground during challenging times. These prayers encourage you to rely on divine guidance and have faith that your business can fulfill a greater purpose.

Adding these prayers to your daily routine can really help you develop integrity, resilience, and gratitude. They can keep you focused and purposeful, even when the highs and lows of business ownership throws some obstacles your way. The verses that follow will provide some extra encouragement, highlighting the strong truth that anyone looking for guidance in their work will always discover it.

1. **Clarity for Vision and Goals**

Heavenly God, thank You for giving me the dream of entrepreneurship. I ask that You grant me clarity for the vision You've placed in my heart. Help me to define my goals with intention and purpose, and to create a roadmap that aligns with Your will. When I feel uncertain or overwhelmed, remind me of the greater purpose behind my business, and let my vision always reflect Your love and grace. Guide my steps as I build and grow, keeping my focus on what truly matters. Amen.

Scripture:

"Commit to the Lord whatever you do, and he will establish your plans."

– Proverbs 16:3

2. **Wisdom for Strategic Decision-Making**

Dear Lord, running a business requires many decisions—some easy, some difficult, and each one has an impact on the direction of my work. Please grant me wisdom and discernment as I navigate each choice, big or small. Let my decisions be strategic, well thought out, and aligned with Your guidance. Give me the insight to know when to act and when to wait, and help me seek wise counsel when needed. May I make choices that honor You and contribute to the success of my business. Amen.

Scripture:

"If any of you lacks wisdom, you should ask God, who gives generously to all without finding fault, and it will be given to you."

— **James 1:5**

3. Faith to Trust in God's Provision

Lord, entrepreneurship often means stepping into the unknown—trusting in the resources, opportunities, and connections that may not yet be visible. In moments of doubt or financial strain, help me to have faith in Your provision. Remind me that You are my provider and that You will meet all of my needs according to Your riches. Let me trust in Your faithfulness and lean on You for every resource, every opportunity, and every bit of support I need to succeed. Amen.

Scripture:

"And my God will meet all your needs according to the riches of his glory in Christ Jesus."

— **Philippians 4:19**

4. Patience for Business Growth

God, I often feel the pressure to see immediate results and quick success. But I know that true growth takes time, hard work, and patience. Please help me to be patient in this journey, to trust the process, and to celebrate the small victories along the way. Let me not become discouraged by slow progress but instead find joy in the steady and faithful work of building something meaningful. Remind me that You are working in the waiting and that good things come to those who persevere. Amen.

Scripture:

"The plans of the diligent lead to profit as surely as haste leads to poverty."

– Proverbs 21:5

5. Strength to Endure Setbacks

Dear God, setbacks are a natural part of the entrepreneurial journey, but they can be discouraging and disheartening. When I face challenges, failures, or disappointments, please give me the strength to endure. Let me see each setback as an opportunity to learn, grow, and come back even stronger. Help me to stay hopeful and resilient, trusting that every obstacle is part of the journey and that You are using these moments to shape me and my business. Amen.

Scripture:

"I can do all this through him who gives me strength."

– Philippians 4:13

6. Gratitude for Opportunities and Challenges

Lord, thank You for the opportunity to be an entrepreneur and to build something from the ground up. I am grateful for the doors You have opened, for the challenges that have made me stronger, and for the growth that has come through each season. Let my heart be filled with gratitude for both the successes and the struggles, knowing that each one has a purpose in shaping my business and my character. May I always approach my work with a spirit of thankfulness. Amen.

Scripture:

"Give thanks in all circumstances; for this is God's will for you in Christ Jesus."

— **1 Thessalonians 5:18**

7. Courage to Take Calculated Risks

Dear God, entrepreneurship requires boldness and the willingness to take risks. Help me to be courageous in my business, to step out in faith when opportunities arise, and to take calculated risks that can lead to growth and success. Let me be wise in my decisions, seeking Your guidance as I navigate the unknown. Remind me that fear has no place in my journey when I am walking in Your will. Amen.

Scripture:

"Have I not commanded you? Be strong and courageous. Do not be afraid; do not be discouraged, for the Lord your God will be with you wherever you go."

— **Joshua 1:9**

8. Perseverance in Difficult Seasons

God, there will be seasons of difficulty, times when progress feels slow, and moments when giving up seems like the easier option. Please help me to persevere in those times, to stay committed to the vision You have given me, and to keep pushing forward even when the road is hard. Let my perseverance be a testament to my faith in You, and may my business be stronger because of the trials we have overcome together. Amen.

Scripture:

"Let us not become weary in doing good, for at the proper time we will reap a harvest if we do not give up."

– Galatians 6:9

9. Peace Amidst Business Uncertainties

Lord, the world of business is full of uncertainties—financial challenges, market fluctuations, and unexpected changes. In the face of these uncertainties, please give me Your peace. Help me to remain calm, centered, and confident, trusting that You are in control and that You have a plan for my business. Let me find peace in Your presence and assurance that I am not alone in this journey. Amen.

Scripture:

"Peace I leave with you; my peace I give you. I do not give to you as the world gives. Do not let your hearts be troubled and do not be afraid."

– John 14:27

10. Integrity in All Business Dealings

Dear God, I want my business to be a reflection of You, a place of honesty, fairness, and integrity. Help me to conduct all my dealings with transparency, to treat every client, partner, and employee with respect, and to make decisions that honor You. Let my business be known for its integrity, and may my actions speak louder than words in demonstrating Your love and righteousness. Amen.

Scripture:

"The righteous person walks in integrity; blessed are his children after him."

— Proverbs 20:7 (ESV)

11. Balance Between Work and Rest

God, as an entrepreneur, it's easy to become consumed by the demands of work and to neglect rest and self-care. Please help me to find a healthy balance between working diligently and taking time to rest and recharge. Let me remember that rest is not a weakness but a necessity and that in order to be my best, I must also take care of my well-being. Teach me to trust that You will take care of my business, even when I step away to rest. Amen.

Scripture:

"Come to me, all you who are weary and burdened, and I will give you rest."

— Matthew 11:28

12. Prayer for Loyal and Supportive Customers

Lord, I am grateful for every customer and client who has supported my business. I pray for continued loyalty and that my business would provide value, quality, and satisfaction to each person it serves. Help me to build strong relationships with my customers, to understand their needs, and to serve them with excellence. Let those who interact with my business leave feeling valued and supported. Amen.

Scripture:

"Let each of you look not only to his own interests, but also to the interests of others."

– Philippians 2:4 (ESV)

13. Confidence in Self and Business Vision

Heavenly God, sometimes I struggle with confidence in myself and in the vision for my business. I question whether I have what it takes and whether my dreams are too big. Please help me to find confidence in You and the calling You've given me. Let me believe in the gifts, talents, and ideas You have placed within me, and let me move forward with boldness and determination. Amen.

Scripture:

"So do not throw away your confidence; it will be richly rewarded."

– Hebrews 10:35

14. Guidance for Ethical and Meaningful Choices

Dear God, as I navigate the daily choices that come with running a business, please guide me in making decisions that are ethical, meaningful, and aligned with Your will. Help me to act with honesty, to treat others with respect, and to prioritize values over profits. Let my business be a place that reflects Your love and principles, and let every decision be made with integrity. Amen.

Scripture:

"The integrity of the upright guides them, but the unfaithful are destroyed by their duplicity."

— Proverbs 11:3

15. Gratitude for Supportive Partners or Team

Lord, I am grateful for the partners, team members, and support system that surround me. I know that building a business is not a solo journey, and I am thankful for those who share in the vision and work alongside me. Help me value and encourage my team, express gratitude for their contributions, and work together in unity toward our shared goals. May our partnership be a blessing to one another and to all those we serve. Amen.

Scripture:

"Two are better than one, because they have a good return for their work: If either of them falls down, one can help the other up."

— Ecclesiastes 4:9-10

16. Empathy for Clients and Employees

Dear God, as I interact with clients and employees, help me to see them as You see them—valuable, unique, and worthy of love and respect. Give me empathy to understand their needs, their struggles, and their dreams. Let me lead with compassion, listen with an open heart, and create a business culture that values people over profits. May my empathy guide my decisions and help me to build strong, lasting relationships with those I serve and work alongside. Amen.

Scripture:

"Be kind and compassionate to one another, forgiving each other, just as in Christ God forgave you."

– Ephesians 4:32

17. Overcoming Fear of Failure

Lord, the fear of failure can be paralyzing, keeping me from taking bold steps and moving forward in my business. Help me to remember that my worth is not defined by my successes or failures but by Your love for me. Let me see failure as an opportunity to learn and grow rather than a reason to give up. Fill me with the courage to take risks, make mistakes, and keep going even when the outcome is uncertain. Help me to trust that You are working in every situation and that even failures can lead to new beginnings. Amen.

Scripture:

"For God has not given us a spirit of fear, but of power and of love and of a sound mind."

– 2 Timothy 1:7 (NKJV)

18. Motivation to Keep Pushing Forward

God, there are times when the road to entrepreneurship feels long and difficult. In those moments, please give me the motivation to keep pushing forward. Help me to remember the passion that inspired me to start this journey and let that passion fuel my determination to continue. Let me find joy in the process, celebrate progress even when it's small, and be encouraged by the impact my business is making. May my drive to succeed be rooted in a desire to serve and honor You. Amen.

Scripture:

"Let us run with perseverance the race marked out for us, fixing our eyes on Jesus, the pioneer and perfecter of faith."

– Hebrews 12:1-

19. Seeking God's Favor in Business Decisions

Dear God, I desire for my business to bring honor and glory to You. As I make decisions and plan for the future, I ask for Your favor over every aspect of my work. Let Your wisdom guide me, let Your hand be upon my business, and let Your favor open doors of opportunity. May my decisions align with Your will, and may my business flourish as a reflection of Your goodness and grace. Amen.

Scripture:

"May the favor of the Lord our God rest on us; establish the work of our hands for us—yes, establish the work of our hands."

– Psalm 90:17

20. Finding Purpose in Serving Others Through Business

Lord, help me to see my business not just as a means of profit, but as a way to serve and bless others. Let my work have a greater purpose beyond financial gain—to create value, meet needs, and make a positive impact in the lives of my clients, employees, and community. Let me find fulfillment in knowing that my business is making a difference and that I am using my gifts and resources to honor You. Amen.

Scripture:

"Each of you should use whatever gift you have received to serve others, as faithful stewards of God's grace in its various forms."

— 1 Peter 4:10

21. Rest for the Mind and Spirit

God, entrepreneurship can be mentally and emotionally draining, and there are days when I feel overwhelmed by stress and responsibility. Please help me to find rest for my mind and spirit, to take time away from work to recharge, and to find peace in Your presence. Let me not be consumed by the demands of business but find balance and rest in You. Teach me to trust that You are in control and that my worth is not tied to my productivity. Amen.

Scripture:

"The Lord is my shepherd; I lack nothing. He makes me lie down in green pastures, he leads me beside quiet waters, he refreshes my soul."

— Psalm 23:1-3

22. Building a Strong Community Around the Business

Dear God, I know that community is essential for the growth and success of my business. Please help me to build strong relationships with my clients, employees, and supporters. Let my business be a place where people feel connected, valued, and supported. Help me to create a culture of inclusivity and belonging, where everyone feels like they are part of something bigger than themselves. May my business foster a sense of community that brings people together and brings glory to You. Amen.

Scripture:

"Therefore encourage one another and build each other up, just as in fact you are doing."

– 1 Thessalonians 5:11

23. Grace in Handling Difficult Customers or Clients

Lord, dealing with difficult clients or customers can be frustrating and challenging. In those moments, help me to respond with grace, patience, and understanding. Let me see beyond their words or actions to the person behind the complaint, and let me address their concerns with empathy and respect. Help me to find peaceful solutions that reflect Your love and care and to handle every situation in a way that honors You. Amen.

Scripture:

"A gentle answer turns away wrath, but a harsh word stirs up anger."

– Proverbs 15:1

24. Thankfulness for Every Small Success

God, in the pursuit of big goals, it's easy to overlook the small wins that happen along the way. Help me to have a heart of gratitude for every step of progress, every new opportunity, and every small success. Let me not take for granted the ways You have blessed and guided my business. Remind me that even the smallest victories are worth celebrating and that each step forward is part of the bigger picture. Let thankfulness overflow from my heart each day. Amen.

Scripture:

"Give thanks to the Lord, for he is good; his love endures forever."

— **Psalm 107:1**

25. Inspiration for New Ideas and Innovation

Dear God, I know that innovation and creativity are crucial for my business to thrive and grow. I pray for fresh inspiration, new ideas, and creative solutions that will set my business apart. Help me to see opportunities where others see obstacles and to dream big dreams that reflect Your creativity. Let Your Spirit guide me in all areas of innovation, and may my ideas bring value and positivity to those my business serves. Amen.

Scripture:

"See, I am doing a new thing! Now it springs up; do you not perceive it? I am making a way in the wilderness and streams in the wasteland."

— **Isaiah 43:19**

26. Trust in God's Timing for Growth

Lord, it can be difficult to wait for growth, especially when it feels like my hard work is not yielding immediate results. Help me to trust in Your timing and to be patient as my business grows according to Your plan. Remind me that You know what is best for my business and that the right opportunities will come at the right time. Let me be faithful in my work, even when the growth is slow, and trust that You are guiding every step. Amen.

Scripture:

"There is a time for everything, and a season for every activity under the heavens."

— Ecclesiastes 3:1

27. Finding Joy in the Entrepreneurial Journey

Dear God, entrepreneurship is a journey filled with ups and downs, successes and failures, excitement and challenges. Help me to find joy in the journey—to savor the learning experiences, to celebrate the growth, and to embrace the process of building something meaningful. Let me not be so focused on the end goal that I miss the joy of the present moment. Help me to see each day as a gift and to find fulfillment in the work You have called me to do. Amen.

Scripture:

"This is the day that the Lord has made; let us rejoice and be glad in it."

— Psalm 118:24

28. Support for Other Entrepreneurs

Lord, as an entrepreneur, I know the challenges, hopes, and dreams that come with this journey. Please help me to be a source of support, encouragement, and inspiration to my fellow business owners. Let me lift others up, share my experiences, and be a positive voice in the entrepreneurial community. May we all work together to build businesses that honor You and make a positive impact in the world. Amen.

Scripture:

"Therefore encourage one another and build each other up, just as in fact you are doing."

— 1 Thessalonians 5:11

29. Developing a Servant-Hearted Leadership Style

God, I want to lead my business not with a desire for power or recognition but with a heart to serve others. Teach me to lead with humility, to put the needs of my clients, employees, and partners before my own, and to make decisions that benefit the greater good. Let my leadership reflect Your servant-hearted nature, and may those who work with me feel valued, respected, and supported. Amen.

Scripture:

"Whoever wants to become great among you must be your servant."

— Matthew 20:26

30. Gratitude for the Privilege to Build and Create

Heavenly God, thank You for the incredible privilege of being an entrepreneur and for the ability to create, build, and pursue a vision. I am grateful for the opportunities to use my gifts, to serve others, and to make a difference through my business. Let me never take for granted the blessing it is to be able to work and create something meaningful. May I always honor You in all that I do, and may my business be a reflection of Your goodness and grace. Amen.

Scripture:

"Whatever you do, work at it with all your heart, as working for the Lord, not for human masters."

— Colossians 3:23

Action Steps For Each Prayer:

- **Clarity for Vision and Goals**

1-Minute Reflection Prompt:

- "What specific goal do I need clarity on today?"

1-Minute Scripture Focus:

- "Commit to the Lord whatever you do, and He will establish your plans." — Proverbs 16:3

1-Minute Personal Prayer:

- "God, I trust You with my vision. I'm grateful for Your guidance. Help me find clarity in my goals today."

Daily Gratitude & Praise Prompt:

- "Today, I found clarity when ____."

Whisper Prayers:

- "Lord, focus my vision."
- **Wisdom for Strategic Decision-Making**

1-Minute Reflection Prompt:

- "What decision requires strategic wisdom today?"

1-Minute Scripture Focus:

- "If any of you lacks wisdom, let him ask of God." — James 1:5

1-Minute Personal Prayer:

- "God, I trust You with my choices. I'm grateful for Your wisdom. Guide my steps in every decision.

Daily Gratitude & Praise Prompt:

- "Today, I felt God's wisdom in ____.

Whisper Prayers:

- "Lord, give me wisdom for today."
- **Faith to Trust in God's Provision**

1-Minute Reflection Prompt:

- "Where can I trust more in God's provision today?

1-Minute Scripture Focus:

- "And my God will supply all your needs according to His riches in glory." — Philippians 4:19

1-Minute Personal Prayer:

- "God, I trust You with my needs. I'm grateful for Your provision. Help me rely fully on You."

Daily Gratitude & Praise Prompt:

- "Today, I trusted God's provision when ____."

Whisper Prayers:

- "Lord, help me trust in Your supply."

4. Patience for Business Growth

1-Minute Reflection Prompt:

- "How can I be patient with my business growth today?"

1-Minute Scripture Focus:

- "Let us not become weary in doing good, for at the proper time we will reap a harvest." — Galatians 6:9

1-Minute Personal Prayer:

- "God, I trust You with the timing of growth. I'm grateful for each step. Help me be patient in this journey."

Daily Gratitude & Praise Prompt:

- "Today, I embraced patience by ____."

Whisper Prayers:

- "Lord, teach me patience in growth."

5. Strength to Endure Setbacks

1-Minute Reflection Prompt:

- "How can I find strength to face challenges today?"

1-Minute Scripture Focus:

- "I can do all things through Christ who strengthens me."
  — Philippians 4:13

1-Minute Personal Prayer:

- "God, I trust You with my struggles. I'm grateful for Your strength. Help me endure setbacks with grace."

Daily Gratitude & Praise Prompt:

- "Today, I found strength when ____."

Whisper Prayers:

- "Lord, give me resilience."

6. Gratitude for Opportunities and Challenges
1-Minute Reflection Prompt:
- "What challenge today can I be grateful for?"

1-Minute Scripture Focus:

- "Give thanks in all circumstances." — 1 Thessalonians 5:18

1-Minute Personal Prayer:

- "God, I trust You with every opportunity. I'm grateful for the challenges that grow me. Help me to stay thankful."

Daily Gratitude & Praise Prompt:

- "Today, I thanked God for ____."

Whisper Prayers:

- "Lord, I am grateful for this challenge."

7. Courage to Take Calculated Risks

1-Minute Reflection Prompt:

- "What risk today requires courage?"

1-Minute Scripture Focus:

- "Be strong and courageous. Do not be afraid." — Joshua 1:9

1-Minute Personal Prayer:

- "God, I trust You with my steps. I'm grateful for Your guidance. Give me the courage to take bold, wise risks."

Daily Gratitude & Praise Prompt:

- "Today, I felt courageous when ____."

Whisper Prayers:

- "Lord, give me the courage to act."

8. Perseverance in Difficult Seasons

1-Minute Reflection Prompt:

- "What challenge requires my perseverance today?"

1-Minute Scripture Focus:

- "Blessed is the one who perseveres under trial." — James 1:12

1-Minute Personal Prayer:

- "God, I trust You with my hardships. I'm grateful for Your strength. Help me persevere through this season."

Daily Gratitude & Praise Prompt:

- "Today, I showed perseverance by ____."

Whisper Prayers:

- "Lord, strengthen me to endure."

9. Peace Amidst Business Uncertainties

1-Minute Reflection Prompt:

- "Where do I need peace in my business today?"

1-Minute Scripture Focus:

- "Peace, I leave with you; my peace I give you." — John 14:27

1-Minute Personal Prayer:

- "God, I trust You with my business. I'm grateful for Your peace. Calm my heart amidst uncertainty."

Daily Gratitude & Praise Prompt:

- "Today, I felt peace when ____."

Whisper Prayers:

- "Lord, grant me peace in this moment."

10. Integrity in All Business Dealings

1-Minute Reflection Prompt:

- "How can I uphold integrity in my work today?"

1-Minute Scripture Focus:

- "The righteous man walks in his integrity." — Proverbs 20:7

1-Minute Personal Prayer:

- "God, I trust You with my character. I'm grateful for Your guidance. Help me act with integrity in every dealing."

Daily Gratitude & Praise Prompt:

- "Today, I practiced integrity when ____."

Whisper Prayers:

- "Lord, keep me honest and true."

11. Balance Between Work and Rest

1-Minute Reflection Prompt:

- "How can I balance work and rest today?"

1-Minute Scripture Focus:

- "There remains, then, a Sabbath-rest for the people of God." — Hebrews 4:9

1-Minute Personal Prayer:

- "God, I trust You with my time. I'm grateful for moments of rest. Help me find a balance between work and renewal."

Daily Gratitude & Praise Prompt:

- "Today, I felt balanced when ____."

Whisper Prayers:

- "Lord, guide me to balance my work."

12. Prayer for Loyal and Supportive Customers

1-Minute Reflection Prompt:

- "How can I show appreciation for my customers today?"

1-Minute Scripture Focus:

- "Serve wholeheartedly, as if you were serving the Lord." — Ephesians 6:7

1-Minute Personal Prayer:

- "God, I trust You with my business relationships. I'm grateful for every loyal customer. Help me serve them well."

Daily Gratitude & Praise Prompt:

- "Today, I appreciated my customers by ____."

Whisper Prayers:

- "Lord, bless those who support my work."

13. Confidence in Self and Business Vision

1-Minute Reflection Prompt:

- "How can I show confidence in my vision today?"

1-Minute Scripture Focus:

- "For the Spirit God gave us does not make us timid, but gives us power." — 2 Timothy 1:7

1-Minute Personal Prayer:

- "God, I trust You with my confidence. I'm grateful for the vision You've given me. Help me to step boldly in faith."

Daily Gratitude & Praise Prompt:

- "Today, I felt confident when ____."

Whisper Prayers:

- "Lord, give me courage to stand firm."

14. Guidance for Ethical and Meaningful Choices

1-Minute Reflection Prompt:

- "What decision requires an ethical focus today?"

1-Minute Scripture Focus:

- "The integrity of the upright guides them." — Proverbs 11:3

1-Minute Personal Prayer:

- "God, I trust You with my decisions. I'm grateful for Your wisdom. Help me make choices that honor You."

Daily Gratitude & Praise Prompt:

- "Today, I made ethical choices when ____."

Whisper Prayers:

- "Lord, guide me to act with integrity."

15. Gratitude for Supportive Partners or Teams

1-Minute Reflection Prompt:

- "How can I appreciate my team or partners today?"

1-Minute Scripture Focus:

- "Therefore encourage one another and build each other up." — 1 Thessalonians 5:11

1-Minute Personal Prayer:

- "God, I trust You with my team. I'm grateful for their support. Help me show them appreciation."

Daily Gratitude & Praise Prompt:

- "Today, I thanked my team by ____."

Whisper Prayers:

- "Lord, thank You for my team's support."

Here are the remaining action steps for each quality:

16. Empathy for Clients and Employees

1-Minute Reflection Prompt:

- "How can I show empathy toward my clients or employees today?"

1-Minute Scripture Focus:

- "Be kind and compassionate to one another." — Ephesians 4:32

1-Minute Personal Prayer:

- "God, I trust You with the people I serve. I'm grateful for Your compassion. Help me to lead with empathy and understanding."

Daily Gratitude & Praise Prompt:

- "Today, I showed empathy by ____."

Whisper Prayers:

- "Lord, help me be compassionate."

17. Overcoming Fear of Failure

1-Minute Reflection Prompt:

- "What fear of failure do I need to release today?"

1-Minute Scripture Focus:

- "For God has not given us a spirit of fear." — 2 Timothy 1:7

1-Minute Personal Prayer:

- "God, I trust You with my fears. I'm grateful for Your strength. Help me let go of the fear of failing."

Daily Gratitude & Praise Prompt:

- "Today, I overcame fear when ____."

Whisper Prayers:

- "Lord, take away my fear of failure."

18. Motivation to Keep Pushing Forward

1-Minute Reflection Prompt:

- "What can I accomplish today to stay motivated?"

1-Minute Scripture Focus:

- "Let us not become weary in doing good." — Galatians 6:9

1-Minute Personal Prayer:

- "God, I trust You with my energy. I'm grateful for each opportunity. Help me stay motivated and focused on my goals."

Daily Gratitude & Praise Prompt:

- "Today, I felt motivated by ____."

Whisper Prayers:

- "Lord, give me the drive to keep going."

19. Seeking God's Favor in Business Decisions

1-Minute Reflection Prompt:

- "What decision today do I seek God's favor for?"

1-Minute Scripture Focus:

- "May the favor of the Lord our God rest on us." — Psalm 90:17

1-Minute Personal Prayer:

- "God, I trust You with my choices. I'm grateful for Your favor. Bless the decisions I make in my business."

Daily Gratitude & Praise Prompt:

- "Today, I sought God's favor in ____."

Whisper Prayers:

- "Lord, let Your favor rest on my work."

20. Finding Purpose in Serving Others Through Business

1-Minute Reflection Prompt:

- "How can I serve others through my work today?"

1-Minute Scripture Focus:

- "Serve wholeheartedly, as if you were serving the Lord." — Ephesians 6:7

1-Minute Personal Prayer:

- "God, I trust You with my purpose. I'm grateful for the chance to serve others. Help me find purpose in each task."

Daily Gratitude & Praise Prompt:

- "Today, I served others by ____."

Whisper Prayers:

- "Lord, help me to serve with joy."

21. Rest for the Mind and Spirit

1-Minute Reflection Prompt:

- "How can I take a moment to rest my mind and spirit today?"

1-Minute Scripture Focus:

- "Come to me, all you who are weary and burdened, and I will give you rest." — Matthew 11:28

1-Minute Personal Prayer:

- "God, I trust You with my rest. I'm grateful for Your peace. Help me find moments to recharge my mind and spirit."

Daily Gratitude & Praise Prompt:

- "Today, I found rest when ____."

Whisper Prayers:

- "Lord, restore my mind and soul."

22. Building a Strong Community Around the Business

1-Minute Reflection Prompt:

- "How can I build relationships in my community today?"

1-Minute Scripture Focus:

- "Let us consider how we may spur one another on toward love and good deeds." — Hebrews 10:24

1-Minute Personal Prayer:

- "God, I trust You with my connections. I'm grateful for my community. Help me to foster strong relationships that uplift everyone."

Daily Gratitude & Praise Prompt:

- "Today, I connected with my community by ____."

Whisper Prayers:

- "Lord, help me build a positive community."

23. Grace in Handling Difficult Customers or Clients

1-Minute Reflection Prompt:

- "How can I approach a challenging customer with grace?"

1-Minute Scripture Focus:

- "Let your conversation be always full of grace." — Colossians 4:6

1-Minute Personal Prayer:

- "God, I trust you with my interactions. I'm grateful for Your grace. Help me show patience and kindness with each person I serve."

Daily Gratitude & Praise Prompt:

- "Today, I handled a difficult situation with grace when _____."

Whisper Prayers:

- "Lord, give me patience and grace."

24. Thankfulness for Every Small Success

1-Minute Reflection Prompt:

- "What small success can I thank God for today?"

1-Minute Scripture Focus:

- "Give thanks in all circumstances." — 1 Thessalonians 5:18

1-Minute Personal Prayer:

- "God, I trust you with every achievement. I'm grateful for each step forward. Help me celebrate the small wins."

Daily Gratitude & Praise Prompt:

- "Today, I thanked God for the success of _____."

Whisper Prayers:

- "Thank You, Lord, for this accomplishment."

25. Inspiration for New Ideas and Innovation

1-Minute Reflection Prompt:

- "Where can I seek fresh inspiration today?"

1-Minute Scripture Focus:

- "Be transformed by the renewing of your mind." — Romans 12:2

1-Minute Personal Prayer:

- "God, I trust you with my creativity. I'm grateful for new ideas. Inspire me to think outside the box and innovate."

Daily Gratitude & Praise Prompt:

- "Today, I felt inspired when ____."

Whisper Prayers:

- "Lord, bless me with creativity today."

26. Trust in God's Timing for Growth

1-Minute Reflection Prompt:

- "How can I trust God's timing for my business today?"

1-Minute Scripture Focus:

- "He has made everything beautiful in its time." — Ecclesiastes 3:11

1-Minute Personal Prayer:

- "God, I trust You with my business's timing. I'm grateful for Your perfect plan. Help me wait patiently for growth."

Daily Gratitude & Praise Prompt:

- "Today, I trusted in God's timing when ____."

Whisper Prayers:

- "Lord, I trust in Your timing."

27. Finding Joy in the Entrepreneurial Journey

1-Minute Reflection Prompt:

- "How can I find joy in my work today?"

1-Minute Scripture Focus:

- "The joy of the Lord is your strength." — Nehemiah 8:10

1-Minute Personal Prayer:

- "God, I trust you with my journey. I'm grateful for each step of this process. Help me to find joy and strength in my work."

Daily Gratitude & Praise Prompt:

- "Today, I felt joy in my work when ____."

Whisper Prayers:

- "Lord, let me find joy in this moment."

28. Support for Other Entrepreneurs

1-Minute Reflection Prompt:

- "How can I encourage or support another entrepreneur today?"

1-Minute Scripture Focus:

- "Therefore, encourage one another and build each other up." — 1 Thessalonians 5:11

1-Minute Personal Prayer:

- "God, I trust you with my network. I'm grateful for fellow entrepreneurs. Help me to encourage and uplift others in their journeys."

Daily Gratitude & Praise Prompt:

- "Today, I supported another entrepreneur by ____."

Whisper Prayers:

- "Lord, let me be an encouragement."

29. Developing a Servant-Hearted Leadership Style

1-Minute Reflection Prompt:

- "How can I serve others through my leadership today?"

1-Minute Scripture Focus:

- "But whoever would be great among you must be your servant." — Matthew 20:26

1-Minute Personal Prayer:

- "God, I trust You with my leadership. I'm grateful for the opportunity to serve. Help me lead with a servant's heart."

Daily Gratitude & Praise Prompt:

- "Today, I served others in my leadership by ____."

Whisper Prayers:

- "Lord, give me a heart of service."

30. Gratitude for the Privilege to Build and Create

1-Minute Reflection Prompt:

- "How can I express gratitude for the chance to create and build today?"

1-Minute Scripture Focus:

- "For we are God's handiwork, created in Christ Jesus to do good works." — Ephesians 2:10

1-Minute Personal Prayer:

- "God, I trust You with my work. I'm grateful for the chance to create something meaningful. Help me use this privilege to make a positive impact."

Daily Gratitude & Praise Prompt:

Chapter Four:
Starting Strong: Prayers for Women Beginning New Chapters

Starting your career can seem a bit difficult. You're balancing new responsibilities, dealing with self-doubt, and figuring out how to stand strong in a fast-paced world. As young professionals, you totally get the pressure of trying to get everything right while also staying true to your values. That's when these prayers really matter.

These prayers aim to provide you with spiritual guidance while you deal the unique challenges of building your career. With heartfelt prayers and uplifting scriptures, you'll discover strength, clarity, and purpose in all that you do. When you're getting through those tough days, welcoming new chances, or keeping your eyes on the bigger picture, these prayers are here to remind you to trust the journey.

This collection is all about embracing gratitude, patience, and trust in God's timing while you take risks, make choices, and expand your connections. Incorporating these prayers into your daily routine can really help you grow in your career while also deepening your faith and sense of purpose.

1. Gratitude for New Opportunities

Heavenly Father, thank You for the opportunities that lie ahead in this new chapter of my life. As I start my career, I am grateful for every door that opens, every connection I make, and every experience that helps me grow. Help me to see each opportunity as a blessing from You, and let me approach my work with a heart full of gratitude. May I honor You in all that I do, and may my career be a path to serve others and fulfill the purpose You have for me. Amen.

Scripture:

"Give thanks to the Lord, for he is good; his love endures forever."

– Psalm 107:1

2. Patience in Career Progression

Lord, sometimes I wish for quick advancement and instant success in my career, but I know that true growth takes time. Please help me to be patient as I progress in my career, to trust in Your timing, and to be faithful in the small steps along the way. Let me not compare my journey to others but instead focus on the path You have laid out for me. May I find contentment in the present while working diligently toward my future goals. Amen.

Scripture:

> *"But let patience have its perfect work, that you may be perfect and complete, lacking nothing."*
>
> *— James 1:4 (NKJV)*

3. Courage to Step Out of Comfort Zones

Dear God, it's easy to stay within the boundaries of what feels safe and familiar, but I know that real growth happens outside of my comfort zone. Please give me the courage to take on new challenges, speak up in meetings, and step into opportunities that may stretch me. Let me be bold in exploring new possibilities, and may my willingness to take risks lead to growth, learning, and new experiences. Amen.

Scripture:

> *"Be strong and courageous. Do not be afraid; do not be discouraged, for the Lord your God will be with you wherever you go."*
>
> *— Joshua 1:9*

4. Wisdom to Make Career Decisions

Father, starting a career comes with many decisions—where to work, what opportunities to pursue, and how to grow professionally. Please give me the wisdom to make choices that align with Your will for my life. Help me to seek counsel from those who are wise, to listen to Your voice, and to trust that You are guiding my steps. Let my decisions lead me to a path that brings purpose, fulfillment, and joy. Amen.

Scripture:

> *"If any of you lacks wisdom, you should ask God, who gives generously to all without finding fault, and it will be given to you."*

– James 1:5

5. Peace Amidst Career Uncertainties

Lord, the beginning of a career can be filled with uncertainties—wondering if I'm in the right place if I'm on the right path, or if I'm truly making a difference. Please grant me peace in these moments of doubt and help me to rest in the knowledge that You have a plan for my life. Let me find comfort in Your presence and trust that You are directing my path even when the future seems unclear. Amen.

Scripture:

"And the peace of God, which transcends all understanding, will guard your hearts and your minds in Christ Jesus."

– Philippians 4:7

6. Motivation to Pursue Personal and Professional Growth

Dear God, I want to grow not only in my career but also as a person. Help me to stay motivated to learn, develop my skills, and become the best version of myself. Let me be proactive in seeking opportunities for personal and professional development, and may I always strive to become the person You created me to be. Inspire me to set goals, seek knowledge, and be diligent in my work. Amen.

Scripture:

"Whatever you do, work at it with all your heart, as working for the Lord, not for human masters."

– Colossians 3:23

7. Joy in Small Accomplishments

Lord, starting a career is a journey made up of many small steps, and sometimes, it's easy to overlook the little wins. Help me to find joy in each accomplishment, no matter how small it may seem. Let me celebrate the progress I make, the lessons I learn, and the opportunities that come my way. May my joy come from the journey, knowing that each step is bringing me closer to fulfilling Your purpose for my life. Amen.

Scripture:

"Rejoice in the Lord always. I will say it again: Rejoice!"

– Philippians 4:4

8. Overcoming Imposter Syndrome

Father, there are times when I feel like I don't belong like I'm not capable, and that others might see through my insecurities. Please help me to overcome imposter syndrome and to stand confidently in the gifts and talents You have given me. Remind me that I am equipped, called, and prepared for this journey and that my worth is not based on my accomplishments but on who I am in You. Let me walk boldly in the identity You have given me. Amen.

Scripture:

"For we are God's handiwork, created in Christ Jesus to do good works, which God prepared in advance for us to do."

– Ephesians 2:10

9. Building Healthy Work Relationships

Dear Lord, as I step into the workplace, help me to build healthy and meaningful relationships with my coworkers. Let me be a person who encourages, uplifts, and supports those around me. Give me the wisdom to communicate well, resolve conflicts with grace, and work as a team player. Let my relationships at work be marked by respect, kindness, and mutual support, and may I reflect Your love in every interaction. Amen.

Scripture:

> *"Do to others as you would have them do to you."*

– Luke 6:31

10. Finding Purpose in Current Roles

Lord, help me to see my current role not just as a job but as a place of purpose and opportunity. Let me find meaning in the work I do each day, and help me to see how it contributes to the greater good. Even in tasks that seem mundane or routine, let me work with a spirit of excellence and joy, knowing that I am serving You in everything I do. Amen.

Scripture:

> *"And whatever you do, whether in word or deed, do it all in the name of the Lord Jesus, giving thanks to God the Father through him."*

– Colossians 3:17

11. Faith to Navigate Career Challenges

Dear God, starting a career comes with its challenges—whether it's learning new skills, facing rejection, or navigating difficult situations. Help me to have faith that You are with me in every challenge and that You will use these moments to grow and refine me. Let me see obstacles not as setbacks, but as opportunities to lean on You and to grow stronger in my faith and my career. Amen.

Scripture:

"I can do all this through him who gives me strength."

– Philippians 4:13

12. Confidence to Take On New Responsibilities

Father, as I grow in my career, new responsibilities and challenges will come my way. Help me to approach these opportunities with confidence, trusting in the skills and abilities You have given me. Let me be bold in accepting new roles and challenges, knowing that You will equip me for every task. Help me to be open to learning, willing to step up, and eager to make a difference. Amen.

Scripture:

"So do not throw away your confidence; it will be richly rewarded."

– Hebrews 10:35

13. Clarity in Defining Career Goals

Lord, there are so many possibilities and paths to take in my career, and sometimes, it's difficult to know which direction to go. Please help me to have clarity as I define my career goals. Let me set intentions that align with Your purpose for my life and that reflect my passions and skills. Guide me as I plan for the future, and let me trust that You are leading me toward the path that is best for me. Amen.

Scripture:

"Commit to the Lord whatever you do, and he will establish your plans."

— Proverbs 16:3

14. Trust in God's Timing for Career Growth

Dear God, I often wish for quick growth and advancement, but I know that Your timing is perfect. Help me to trust in Your plan for my career, to be patient in the waiting, and to embrace every season as an opportunity for growth. Let me not rush the process but trust that You are shaping me for something greater. May I find peace in knowing that You are in control of my future. Amen.

Scripture:

"There is a time for everything, and a season for every activity under the heavens."

— Ecclesiastes 3:1

15. Balance Between Work and Self-Care

Lord, as I start my career, help me to find a healthy balance between work and taking care of myself. Let me not become consumed by my job to the point of neglecting my health, relationships, and spiritual life. Teach me to rest when I need it, to find joy outside of work, and to maintain a balanced lifestyle that allows me to thrive in all areas of life. Amen.

Scripture:

"Do you not know that your bodies are temples of the Holy Spirit, who is in you, whom you have received from God? You are not your own."

— **1 Corinthians 6:19**

16. Resilience to Face Rejection or Setbacks

Father, as I navigate the beginning of my career, I know there will be times of rejection, failure, and setbacks. Please help me to be resilient, to bounce back from disappointments, and to keep moving forward with hope and determination. Let me see these moments as opportunities for growth, and may I find strength in You to overcome any challenges that come my way. Amen.

Scripture:

"Not only so, but we also glory in our sufferings, because we know that suffering produces perseverance; perseverance, character; and character, hope."

— **Romans 5:3-4**

17. Gratitude for Mentors and Guides

Dear God, thank You for the mentors, guides, and role models who have helped me along my journey. I am grateful for their wisdom, encouragement, and support. Help me to learn from their experiences, to value their advice, and to be open to their guidance. Let me express my gratitude for the impact they have had on my life, and may I someday have the opportunity to pour into others as they have poured into me. Amen.

Scripture:

"Plans fail for lack of counsel, but with many advisers they succeed."

– Proverbs 15:22

18. Hope in Finding the Right Career Path

Lord, there are times when I feel uncertain about my career path and wonder if I'm headed in the right direction. Please fill me with hope and confidence that You are guiding my steps. Let me trust that You have a plan for my life and that You are leading me toward the right opportunities. Help me to stay hopeful and to keep moving forward, knowing that You will place me where I need to be. Amen.

Scripture:

"For I know the plans I have for you,' declares the Lord, 'plans to prosper you and not to harm you, plans to give you hope and a future."

– Jeremiah 29:11

19. Developing a Positive Work Ethic

Father, as I grow in my career, help me to develop a positive work ethic—to work diligently, with integrity, and with a spirit of excellence. Let me be a person who shows up on time, gives my best effort, and serves as an example to others. May my work ethic reflect Your character and bring glory to You. Amen.

Scripture:

"The diligent find freedom in their work; the lazy are oppressed by work."

– Proverbs 12:24 (MSG)

20. Self-Worth Beyond Job Titles or Roles

Dear Lord, remind me that my worth is not defined by my job title, my salary, or my achievements. Help me to find my identity in You and to know that I am valuable simply because I am Your child. Let me approach my work with passion and dedication, but let me not place my self-worth in what I do. Help me to see that my value comes from who I am in You. Amen.

Scripture:

"For you created my inmost being; you knit me together in my mother's womb. I praise you because I am fearfully and wonderfully made; your works are wonderful; I know that full well."

– Psalm 139:13-14

21. Patience in Learning New Skills

Lord, starting a new career often means learning new skills, systems, and knowledge. Please help me to be patient with myself as I learn and grow. Let me approach every new lesson with humility and a willingness to learn, knowing that growth takes time. Help me to seek improvement each day, to ask for help when needed, and to trust that You will equip me with what I need to succeed. Amen.

Scripture:

"Instruct the wise and they will be wiser still; teach the righteous and they will add to their learning."

– Proverbs 9:9

22. Seeing Work as a Form of Service

Father, help me to see my work not just as a means to earn a living but as a way to serve others. Let me approach my tasks with a servant's heart, seeking to bring value, encouragement, and support to those I interact with. May my work be a reflection of Your love and grace, and may I find fulfillment in serving others through what I do. Amen.

Scripture:

"Each of you should use whatever gift you have received to serve others, as faithful stewards of God's grace in its various forms."

– 1 Peter 4:10

23. Honesty in All Work and Relationships

Dear God, as I navigate the workplace, help me to always act with honesty and integrity. Let my words be truthful, my actions transparent, and my relationships marked by trust and respect. Help me to build a reputation for being honest and dependable, and let me honor You in all my dealings. Amen.

Scripture:

"The Lord detests lying lips, but he delights in people who are trustworthy."

– Proverbs 12:22

24. Prayer for Professional Growth and Success

Lord, I desire to grow and succeed in my career, not just for personal gain but to make a positive impact and to use my talents for Your glory. Please guide my steps toward opportunities for growth, advancement, and success. Let my work be fruitful, and may I use every blessing You provide to serve others and honor You. Amen.

Scripture:

"Commit to the Lord whatever you do, and he will establish your plans."

– Proverbs 16:3

25. Overcoming Feelings of Overwhelm

Dear God, there are days when the demands of my job feel overwhelming, and I struggle to keep up with the responsibilities and expectations placed on me. Please calm my anxious heart, help me prioritize my tasks, and grant me the strength to take things one step at a time. Let me find peace in Your presence and trust that You will provide everything I need to succeed. Amen.

Scripture:

"Cast all your anxiety on him because he cares for you."

– 1 Peter 5:7

26. Encouragement to Continue Striving for Excellence

Lord, help me to approach my work with a spirit of excellence. Let me be encouraged to give my best effort, to continue learning and improving, and to strive for high standards in all that I do. May my work reflect a heart of dedication and a desire to serve others well. Let me not settle for mediocrity but seek to honor You through my commitment to excellence. Amen.

Scripture:

"Whatever you do, work at it with all your heart, as working for the Lord, not for human masters."

– Colossians 3:23

27. Building Trust and Respect with Coworkers

Father, relationships in the workplace are crucial to a positive work environment. Help me to build trust and respect with my coworkers, to communicate well, and to work as a team. Let me be reliable, honest, and supportive, and may my actions contribute to a healthy and uplifting work culture. May I reflect Your love in every relationship I build. Amen.

Scripture:

"Be devoted to one another in love. Honor one another above yourselves."

– Romans 12:10

28. Joy in Contributing to Team Success

Dear God, thank You for the opportunity to be part of a team, to work alongside others, and to contribute to something greater than myself. Help me to find joy in teamwork and collaboration, to celebrate the successes of my team members, and to work together toward shared goals. Let me be a source of encouragement and support, and may our teamwork bring glory to You. Amen.

Scripture:

"Rejoice with those who rejoice; mourn with those who mourn."

– Romans 12:15

29. Seeking God's Guidance in Career Steps

Lord, as I take steps forward in my career, help me to seek Your guidance in every decision, opportunity, and path. Let me be sensitive to Your leading, listen for Your voice, and follow the path that aligns with Your will. May my career be a journey of faith, trusting that You are guiding my steps and that You have a purpose for my life. Amen.

Scripture:

"Your word is a lamp for my feet, a light on my path."

– Psalm 119:105

30. Gratitude for the Journey of Starting a Career

Heavenly Father, thank You for this journey of starting my career. I am grateful for every lesson, every opportunity, every challenge, and every moment that has shaped me. Help me to approach each day with a heart of gratitude, to be thankful for the growth and progress I've made, and to look forward to the future with hope and excitement. Let my career be a reflection of Your goodness and grace, and may I always honor You in all that I do. Amen.

Scripture:

"Rejoice always, pray continually, give thanks in all circumstances; for this is God's will for you in Christ Jesus."

– 1 Thessalonians 5:16-18

Action Steps For Each Prayer:

1. Gratitude for New Opportunities

1-Minute Reflection Prompt:

- "What opportunity am I thankful for today?"

1-Minute Scripture Focus:

- "Every good and perfect gift is from above." — James 1:17

1-Minute Personal Prayer:

- "God, thank You for the doors You've opened. Help me to embrace these opportunities with gratitude and purpose."

Daily Gratitude & Praise Prompt:

- "Today, I felt gratitude for an opportunity to ____."

Whisper Prayer:

- "Lord, thank You for new beginnings."

2. Patience in Career Progression

1-Minute Reflection Prompt:

- "Where do I need patience in my career journey today?"

1-Minute Scripture Focus:

- "Wait for the Lord; be strong and take heart." — Psalm 27:14

1-Minute Personal Prayer:

- "God, I trust Your timing. Help me to wait patiently and focus on growing where I am now."

Daily Gratitude & Praise Prompt:

- "Today, I practiced patience by ____."

Whisper Prayer:

- "Lord, teach me patience in Your plan."

3. Courage to Step Out of Comfort Zones

1-Minute Reflection Prompt:

- "What challenge can I face with courage today?"

1-Minute Scripture Focus:

- "Be strong and courageous. Do not be afraid." — Joshua 1:9

1-Minute Personal Prayer:

- "God, give me the courage to step forward in faith. Help me to trust You even when I feel uncertain."

Daily Gratitude & Praise Prompt:

- "Today, I found the courage to ____."

Whisper Prayer:

- "Lord, strengthen my heart."

4. Wisdom to Make Career Decisions

1-Minute Reflection Prompt:

- "What decision requires wisdom today?"

1-Minute Scripture Focus:

- "If any of you lacks wisdom, let him ask of God." — James 1:5

1-Minute Personal Prayer:

- "God, guide me with Your wisdom. Help me make decisions that align with Your plan for me."

Daily Gratitude & Praise Prompt:

- "Today, I felt God's wisdom when _____."

Whisper Prayer:

- "Lord, lead me with wisdom."

5. Peace Amidst Career Uncertainties

1-Minute Reflection Prompt:

- "Where do I need peace in my career today?"

1-Minute Scripture Focus:

- "The peace of God... will guard your hearts and your minds." — Philippians 4:7

1-Minute Personal Prayer:

- "God, calm my worries and fill me with peace. Help me trust You even in the unknown."

Daily Gratitude & Praise Prompt:

- "Today, I felt peace about _____."

Whisper Prayer:

- "Lord, give me Your peace."

6. Motivation to Pursue Growth

1-Minute Reflection Prompt:

- "What goal can I work toward with motivation today?"

1-Minute Scripture Focus:

- "Whatever you do, work heartily, as for the Lord." — Colossians 3:23

1-Minute Personal Prayer:

- "God, give me the motivation to pursue growth and excellence. Help me to work with purpose and joy."

Daily Gratitude & Praise Prompt:

- "Today, I felt motivated to ____."

Whisper Prayer:

- "Lord, renew my energy."

7. Joy in Small Accomplishments

1-Minute Reflection Prompt:

- "What small win can I celebrate today?"

1-Minute Scripture Focus:

- "Rejoice always." — 1 Thessalonians 5:16

1-Minute Personal Prayer:

- "God, help me find joy in the little things. Thank You for every step forward, no matter how small."

Daily Gratitude & Praise Prompt:

- "Today, I found joy in ____."

Whisper Prayer:

- "Lord, thank You for progress."

8. Overcoming Imposter Syndrome

1-Minute Reflection Prompt:

- "What truth about myself do I need to embrace today?"

1-Minute Scripture Focus:

- "I am fearfully and wonderfully made." — Psalm 139:14

1-Minute Personal Prayer:

- "God, remind me of my worth. Help me to see myself as You see me and let go of self-doubt."

Daily Gratitude & Praise Prompt:

- "Today, I overcame self-doubt by ____."

Whisper Prayer:

- "Lord, help me see my value."

9. Building Healthy Work Relationships

1-Minute Reflection Prompt:

- "How can I strengthen a relationship at work today?"

1-Minute Scripture Focus:

- "Be kind and compassionate to one another." — Ephesians 4:32

1-Minute Personal Prayer:

- "God, help me to connect with others in a way that reflects Your love. Build trust and kindness in my work relationships."

Daily Gratitude & Praise Prompt:

- "Today, I built a stronger connection with ____."

Whisper Prayer:

- "Lord, guide me in relationships."

10. Finding Purpose in Current Roles

1-Minute Reflection Prompt:

- "How can I bring purpose to my work today?"

1-Minute Scripture Focus:

- "And whatever you do, do it with all your heart." — Colossians 3:23

1-Minute Personal Prayer:

- "God, show me the purpose in my work today. Help me to honor You in everything I do."

Daily Gratitude & Praise Prompt:

- "Today, I found purpose in ____."

Whisper Prayer:

- "Lord, align my work with Your will."

11. Faith to Navigate Career Challenges

1-Minute Reflection Prompt:

- "What challenge do I need faith to face today?"

1-Minute Scripture Focus:

- "Walk by faith, not by sight." — 2 Corinthians 5:7

1-Minute Personal Prayer:

- "God, strengthen my faith to trust You in the challenges I face. Help me see that You are working all things for my good."

Daily Gratitude & Praise Prompt:

- "Today, I found faith to trust God with ____."

Whisper Prayer:

- "Lord, help me walk by faith."

12. Confidence to Take on New Responsibilities

1-Minute Reflection Prompt:

- "What responsibility can I approach with confidence today?"

1-Minute Scripture Focus:

- "The Lord is my helper; I will not be afraid." — Hebrews 13:6

1-Minute Personal Prayer:

- "God, help me embrace new responsibilities with courage and confidence, trusting in Your guidance."

Daily Gratitude & Praise Prompt:

- "Today, I felt confident in ____."

Whisper Prayer:

- "Lord, give me boldness."

13. Clarity in Defining Career Goals

1-Minute Reflection Prompt:

- "What career goal needs more clarity today?"

1-Minute Scripture Focus:

- "Your word is a lamp to my feet and a light to my path." — Psalm 119:105

1-Minute Personal Prayer:

- "God, illuminate my path. Help me clearly define my goals and take steps toward them with focus and intention."

Daily Gratitude & Praise Prompt:

- "Today, I gained clarity on ____."

Whisper Prayer:

- "Lord, guide my vision."

14. Trust in God's Timing for Career Growth

1-Minute Reflection Prompt:

- "Where do I need to trust God's timing in my career?"

1-Minute Scripture Focus:

- "He has made everything beautiful in its time." — Ecclesiastes 3:11

1-Minute Personal Prayer:

- "God, help me trust Your perfect timing. Teach me to wait with patience and faith."

Daily Gratitude & Praise Prompt:

- "Today, I trusted God's timing in ____."

Whisper Prayer:

- "Lord, I trust Your timing."

15. Balance Between Work and Self-Care

1-Minute Reflection Prompt:

- "What can I do today to prioritize self-care?"

1-Minute Scripture Focus:

- "Come to me, all you who are weary and burdened, and I will give you rest." — Matthew 11:28

1-Minute Personal Prayer:

- "God, help me find a balance between my work and caring for myself. Teach me to rest in You."

Daily Gratitude & Praise Prompt:

- "Today, I created balance by ____."

Whisper Prayer:

- "Lord, help me find balance."

16. Resilience to Face Rejection or Setbacks

1-Minute Reflection Prompt:

- "What rejection or setback can I overcome today?"

1-Minute Scripture Focus:

- "We rejoice in our sufferings, knowing that suffering produces endurance." — Romans 5:3

1-Minute Personal Prayer:

- "God, give me resilience to face challenges with strength and hope. Help me see rejection as a step toward growth."

Daily Gratitude & Praise Prompt:

- "Today, I grew stronger by overcoming ____."

Whisper Prayer:

- "Lord, make me resilient."

17. Gratitude for Mentors and Guides

1-Minute Reflection Prompt:

- "Who can I express gratitude to for their guidance today?"

1-Minute Scripture Focus:

- "The wise store up knowledge." — Proverbs 10:14

1-Minute Personal Prayer:

- "God, thank You for the people You've placed in my life to guide and mentor me. Help me to appreciate and learn from them."

Daily Gratitude & Praise Prompt:

- "Today, I showed gratitude for ____."

Whisper Prayer:

- "Lord, thank You for those who guide me."

18. Hope in Finding the Right Career Path

1-Minute Reflection Prompt:

- "Where do I need hope in my career journey today?"

1-Minute Scripture Focus:

- "For I know the plans I have for you, declares the Lord." — Jeremiah 29:11

1-Minute Personal Prayer:

- "God, fill me with hope as I walk the path You've set for me. Help me trust that You are leading me to the right place."

Daily Gratitude & Praise Prompt:

- "Today, I found hope in ____."

Whisper Prayer:

- "Lord, renew my hope."

19. Developing a Positive Work Ethic

1-Minute Reflection Prompt:

- "How can I approach my work with integrity today?"

1-Minute Scripture Focus:

- "Whatever you do, work at it with all your heart." — Colossians 3:23

1-Minute Personal Prayer:

- "God, help me develop a strong and positive work ethic. Let my efforts honor You and inspire others."

Daily Gratitude & Praise Prompt:

- "Today, I honored God through my work by ____."

Whisper Prayer:

- "Lord, guide my efforts."

20. Self-Worth Beyond Job Titles or Roles

1-Minute Reflection Prompt:

- "Where am I finding my value today?"

1-Minute Scripture Focus:

- "You are precious in my eyes and honored, and I love you." — Isaiah 43:4

1-Minute Personal Prayer:

- "God, remind me that my worth comes from You, not my career or accomplishments. Help me rest in that truth."

Daily Gratitude & Praise Prompt:

- "Today, I felt worthy because ____."

Whisper Prayer:

- "Lord, help me see my value in You."

21. Patience in Learning New Skills

1-Minute Reflection Prompt:

- "What skill am I growing in today?"

1-Minute Scripture Focus:

- "Let perseverance finish its work so that you may be mature and complete." — James 1:4

1-Minute Personal Prayer:

- "God, give me patience as I learn and grow. Help me embrace the process with perseverance."

Daily Gratitude & Praise Prompt:

- "Today, I made progress in learning ____."

Whisper Prayer:

- "Lord, strengthen my patience."

22. Seeing Work as a Form of Service

1-Minute Reflection Prompt:

- "How can I serve others through my work today?"

1-Minute Scripture Focus:

- "Serve wholeheartedly, as if you were serving the Lord." — Ephesians 6:7

1-Minute Personal Prayer:

- "God, show me how my work can be a blessing to others. Help me to serve with joy and humility."

Daily Gratitude & Praise Prompt:

- "Today, I served others by ____."

Whisper Prayer:

- "Lord, let my work glorify You."

23. Honesty in All Work and Relationships

1-Minute Reflection Prompt:

- "Where do I need to practice honesty today?"

1-Minute Scripture Focus:

- "The integrity of the upright guides them." — Proverbs 11:3

1-Minute Personal Prayer:

- "God, help me to always act with integrity and honesty in my work and relationships."

Daily Gratitude & Praise Prompt:

- "Today, I honored honesty by ____."

Whisper Prayer:

- "Lord, keep me grounded in truth."

24. Prayer for Professional Growth and Success

1-Minute Reflection Prompt:

- "Where do I seek God's help for growth today?"

1-Minute Scripture Focus:

- "Commit to the Lord whatever you do, and He will establish your plans." — Proverbs 16:3

1-Minute Personal Prayer:

- "God, guide me in my professional growth. Help me achieve success that aligns with Your purpose for my life."

Daily Gratitude & Praise Prompt:

- "Today, I grew professionally by ____."

Whisper Prayer:

- "Lord, establish my plans."

25. Overcoming Feelings of Overwhelm

1-Minute Reflection Prompt:

- "What is overwhelming me, and how can I trust God with it today?"

1-Minute Scripture Focus:

- "Cast all your anxiety on Him because He cares for you." — 1 Peter 5:7

1-Minute Personal Prayer:

- "God, help me release my overwhelm and trust You to carry the weight. Fill me with peace and strength."

Daily Gratitude & Praise Prompt:

- "Today, I overcame overwhelm by _____."

Whisper Prayer:

- "Lord, calm my spirit."

26. Encouragement to Strive for Excellence

1-Minute Reflection Prompt:

- "What task can I approach with excellence today?"

1-Minute Scripture Focus:

- "Do you see someone skilled in their work? They will serve before kings." — Proverbs 22:29

1-Minute Personal Prayer:

- "God, inspire me to strive for excellence in all I do. Help me give my best effort, knowing it reflects You."

Daily Gratitude & Praise Prompt:

- "Today, I gave my best effort in ____."

Whisper Prayer:

- "Lord, empower my work."

27. Building Trust and Respect with Coworkers

1-Minute Reflection Prompt:

- "How can I build trust and respect at work today?"

1-Minute Scripture Focus:

- "So, in everything, do to others what you would have them do to you." — Matthew 7:12

1-Minute Personal Prayer:

- "God, help me to be trustworthy and respectful in all my interactions. Let me reflect Your love to others."

Daily Gratitude & Praise Prompt:

- "Today, I built trust by ____."

Whisper Prayer:

- "Lord, guide my relationships."

28. Joy in Contributing to Team Success

1-Minute Reflection Prompt:

- "How can I contribute to my team's success today?"

1-Minute Scripture Focus:

- "Two are better than one, because they have a good return for their labor." — Ecclesiastes 4:9

1-Minute Personal Prayer:

- "God, help me to be a team player and find joy in helping others succeed."

Daily Gratitude & Praise Prompt:

- "Today, I contributed to my team by ____."

Whisper Prayer:

- "Lord, use me to build others up."

29. Seeking God's Guidance in Career Steps

1-Minute Reflection Prompt:

- "What step do I need God's guidance on today?"

1-Minute Scripture Focus:

- "Trust in the Lord with all your heart and lean not on your own understanding." — Proverbs 3:5

1-Minute Personal Prayer:

- "God, guide me in my career journey. Help me trust Your leading and follow where You take me."

Daily Gratitude & Praise Prompt:

- "Today, I felt God's guidance when ____."

Whisper Prayer:

- "Lord, show me the way."

30. Gratitude for the Journey of Starting a Career

1-Minute Reflection Prompt:

- "What part of my career journey am I thankful for today?"

1-Minute Scripture Focus:

- "Give thanks in all circumstances." — 1 Thessalonians 5:18

1-Minute Personal Prayer:

- "God, thank You for every step of this career journey. Help me to see the lessons and blessings in it all."

Daily Gratitude & Praise Prompt:

- "Today, I felt grateful for ____ in my career."

Whisper Prayer:

- "Lord, thank You for this journey."

Chapter Five:
Finding Purpose: Prayers for Women Embracing Life Transitions

This chapter is for you—the woman figuring out the ups and downs of a career change. It's a time of change, and with that, there's a blend of excitement, uncertainty, and occasionally a bit of fear. Every prayer here is crafted to provide you with strength, peace, and guidance as you step into this new chapter of your life.

When change feels like too much to handle, taking a moment to pray for trust in God's plan can really help. It's a reminder that even if things aren't going the way you expected, they're still part of a bigger picture. When one door closes, it usually means another one is opening up, and often just when you need it most.

Sometimes, the fear of what we don't know can really stop us from grabbing new chances. When you pray for courage, it's a gentle nudge to move ahead, even if you're feeling a bit unsure. Just remember, you're not on this journey by yourself—God is right there with you every step of the way.

In certain instances, you might feel a bit impatient or start to doubt things. The prayers for patience and clarity really provide some comfort, reminding you that God is always at work behind the scenes, guiding you even when the whole picture isn't clear. Just believe that everything is happening the way it's meant to.

Deciding what to do during a transition can be challenging, but taking a moment to pray for wisdom can really help you find the clarity you need to make choices that fit with your purpose. Just a little nudge to look for guidance and believe that each step you take is getting you closer to what you're really meant to do

When you think about your past roles, taking a moment to express gratitude helps you appreciate the lessons you've picked up along the way. Every experience and skill you pick up is like a stepping stone, getting you ready for what's coming next.

Finally, this prayer for resilience is an encouraging reminder to keep pushing forward, even when things get tough. Rejection and challenges aren't failures; they're actually chances for us to grow. This chapter is all about helping you through your career transition with a sense of faith, hope, and strength. Remember, every new beginning is an opportunity for more fulfillment in both your personal and professional life.

1. Trust in God's Plan for Change

Heavenly Father, as I navigate this season of career transition, help me to trust in Your plan for my life. I know that change can be uncertain and unsettling, but I believe that You are guiding my steps. Help me to lean on Your wisdom and to trust that You have a purpose for every door that opens and every door that closes. May I find peace in knowing that You are in control, and let me rest in the assurance that Your plan is good. Amen.

Scripture:

"For I know the plans I have for you,' declares the Lord, 'plans to prosper you and not to harm you, plans to give you hope and a future."

— **Jeremiah 29:11**

2. Courage to Embrace New Opportunities

Dear God, new opportunities often come with uncertainty, fear, and risk. Please grant me the courage to embrace these opportunities with an open heart and a willing spirit. Let me not shy away from what is unfamiliar, but instead see it as an adventure and a chance to grow. Help me to boldly step out in faith, trusting that You are leading me into something greater. Amen.

Scripture:

"Have I not commanded you? Be strong and courageous. Do not be afraid; do not be discouraged, for the Lord your God will be with you wherever you go."

— **Joshua 1:9**

3. Faith in the Process of Transition

Lord, change is not always easy, and the process of transitioning from one season to another can be challenging. Help me to have faith in the process, to know that even when things seem uncertain, You are working behind the scenes. Let me embrace the journey with patience and hope, knowing that every step is part of Your greater plan for my life. Amen.

Scripture:

"Now faith is confidence in what we hope for and assurance about what we do not see."

– Hebrews 11:1

4. Wisdom to Make Sound Decisions

Father, as I face new choices and decisions in my career, I ask for Your wisdom and discernment. Help me to make sound decisions that align with Your will for my life and that lead me closer to the purpose You have set for me. Guide my thoughts, give me clarity, and help me to seek wise counsel when needed. May my decisions bring honor to You. Amen.

Scripture:

"If any of you lacks wisdom, you should ask God, who gives generously to all without finding fault, and it will be given to you."

– James 1:5

5. Gratitude for the Lessons Learned in Past Roles

Dear God, I am grateful for every role and experience that has brought me to this point. Thank You for the lessons I've learned, the skills I've gained, and the people who have shaped me along the way. Help me to carry these lessons with me into the next chapter of my career, knowing that each experience has prepared me for what's ahead. Let my heart be filled with gratitude for the past and hope for the future. Amen.

Scripture:

"Give thanks in all circumstances; for this is God's will for you in Christ Jesus."

— 1 Thessalonians 5:18

6. Patience During Periods of Uncertainty

Lord, transition can be filled with uncertainty, and it's easy to become anxious or impatient during this time. Help me to find patience in the waiting, to trust that You are working even when things are not clear. Teach me to embrace the process, to find peace in the present moment, and to wait on You with a hopeful heart. Amen.

Scripture:

"Be still before the Lord and wait patiently for him; do not fret when people succeed in their ways, when they carry out their wicked schemes."

— Psalm 37:7

7. Strength to Face Fears of the Unknown

Father, stepping into something new can be scary, and there are times when I am overwhelmed by the fear of the unknown. Please give me the strength to face these fears head-on, to trust that You are with me every step of the way, and to know that I am not alone in this journey. Let my faith be stronger than my fear, and let me walk boldly into the future You have prepared for me. Amen.

Scripture:

"So do not fear, for I am with you; do not be dismayed, for I am your God. I will strengthen you and help you; I will uphold you with my righteous right hand."

— **Isaiah 41:10**

8. Seeking Clarity in New Directions

Dear God, as I seek to understand where You are leading me in this new season, please give me clarity and vision. Let me see the path You have set before me, and help me to discern the right opportunities and directions to take. Open my eyes to see possibilities I may have overlooked and guide me toward a career path that brings fulfillment and purpose. Amen.

Scripture:

"Your word is a lamp for my feet, a light on my path."

— **Psalm 119:105**

9. Peace Amidst Anxiety Over Changes

Lord, the thought of change can bring anxiety, worry, and stress. Help me to find peace amidst these changes, to cast my cares on You, and to trust that You are leading me to something good. Let Your peace calm my anxious heart and help me to navigate this season with a spirit of trust and surrender. Amen.

Scripture:

"Do not be anxious about anything, but in every situation, by prayer and petition, with thanksgiving, present your requests to God. And the peace of God, which transcends all understanding, will guard your hearts and your minds in Christ Jesus."

– Philippians 4:6-7

10. Grace in Handling Unexpected Detours

Father, transitions do not always go as planned, and sometimes unexpected detours and challenges arise. Help me to handle these moments with grace, to see the opportunities in the obstacles, and to trust that You are using every situation for my good. Let me be flexible and open to Your redirection, knowing that You are guiding my steps even when the path changes. Amen.

Scripture:

"And we know that in all things God works for the good of those who love him, who have been called according to his purpose."

– Romans 8:28

11. Self-confidence to Try Something New

Dear Lord, starting something new can be daunting, and I often question whether I am capable or qualified. Please give me the self-confidence to step into new roles, try new things, and believe in the gifts and talents You have given me. Let me find confidence not in my own abilities but in Your strength and the purpose You have for my life. Amen.

Scripture:

"I can do all this through him who gives me strength."

– Philippians 4:13

12. Perspective to See Opportunities, Not Setbacks

Father, when things don't go as planned or challenges arise, help me to see these moments not as setbacks but as opportunities for growth and redirection. Give me a positive perspective to see the silver lining in every situation and to trust that You are leading me to something better. Let me be open to the opportunities that come my way, even when they look different from what I expected. Amen.

Scripture:

"Consider it pure joy, my brothers and sisters, whenever you face trials of many kinds because you know that the testing of your faith produces perseverance."

– James 1:2-3

13. Support from Friends and Family During Transitions

Dear God, thank You for the support of friends and family during this season of change. I am grateful for their encouragement, advice, and love. Help me to lean on them when I need support and to be open to the help they offer. Let me also be a source of encouragement to others who may be going through transitions, and may we all grow stronger together. Amen.

Scripture:

"Carry each other's burdens, and in this way, you will fulfill the law of Christ."

– Galatians 6:2

14. Trust in God's Perfect Timing

Lord, sometimes I want things to happen quickly, and I struggle to be patient in waiting for Your timing. Help me to trust that Your timing is perfect and that You know what is best for me. Let me surrender my own timeline and embrace the journey You have set before me, knowing that You will open doors when the time is right. Amen.

Scripture:

"He has made everything beautiful in its time."

– Ecclesiastes 3:11

15. Letting Go of What No Longer Serves Them

Dear God, as I move forward in this new season, help me to let go of the things that no longer serve me—whether they are old habits, mindsets, or roles that are holding me back. Give me the courage to release what is not beneficial and to make room for the new opportunities and growth that You have prepared for me. Let me trust that letting go is not a loss but a step toward something greater. Amen.

Scripture:

"Forget the former things; do not dwell on the past. See, I am doing a new thing!"

– Isaiah 43:18-19

16. Joy in the New Experiences Ahead

Father, as I embark on this new journey, let my heart be filled with joy and excitement for the experiences that lie ahead. Help me to embrace each day with a sense of wonder and anticipation, knowing that You are leading me to a place of growth, learning, and fulfillment. Let me find joy in the journey and trust that every step is part of a greater story. Amen.

Scripture:

"This is the day that the Lord has made; let us rejoice and be glad in it."

– Psalm 118:24

17. Prayer for Finding the Right Opportunities

Dear Lord, as I search for new opportunities, please guide me to the ones that are right for me—opportunities that align with my passions, skills, and purpose. Let me be patient in the search, open to Your leading, and willing to step into the roles You have prepared for me. May I find doors that lead to fulfillment and growth, and may my work bring glory to You. Amen.

Scripture:

"Ask and it will be given to you; seek and you will find; knock and the door will be opened to you."

– Matthew 7:7

18. Resilience in Handling Rejections or Delays

Father, I know that not every opportunity will work out, and there may be times of rejection, delays, and disappointment. Please give me the resilience to keep moving forward, to learn from every experience, and to remain hopeful even in the face of setbacks. Let me see rejections as redirection, and may I trust that You are leading me to the right place in Your perfect timing. Amen.

Scripture:

"Let us not become weary in doing good, for at the proper time, we will reap a harvest if we do not give up."

– Galatians 6:9

19. Seeking a Deeper Purpose in Work

Lord, I desire for my work to be more than just a job—I want it to have meaning, impact, and purpose. Help me to seek out opportunities that allow me to use my gifts to make a difference, to serve others, and to fulfill the purpose You have placed in my heart. Let my work be a reflection of Your love, grace, and goodness. Amen.

Scripture:

"Whatever you do, work at it with all your heart, as working for the Lord, not for human masters."

– Colossians 3:23

20. Finding Community and Support in New Roles

Dear God, as I step into new roles and environments, help me to find a sense of community and belonging. Let me connect with others who share my values and goals, and let us support one another in our journey. Help me to be a source of encouragement to my colleagues, and may we all grow together in a spirit of unity and respect. Amen.

Scripture:

"Therefore encourage one another and build each other up, just as in fact you are doing."

– 1 Thessalonians 5:11

21. Overcoming Self-Doubt

Father, during times of transition, it's easy to doubt my abilities and question whether I am on the right path. Please help me to overcome self-doubt and to remember that I am fearfully and wonderfully made. Let me find confidence in the gifts and talents You have given me, and let me trust that You have called me to this new season for a reason. Amen.

Scripture:

"I praise you because I am fearfully and wonderfully made; your works are wonderful; I know that full well."

– Psalm 139:14

22. Embracing New Challenges with Faith

Dear God, I know that every new opportunity comes with its own set of challenges and unknowns. Help me to embrace these challenges with faith, knowing that You are equipping me with the strength and wisdom I need to succeed. Let me not be intimidated by what is unfamiliar, but instead see every challenge as a chance to grow and learn. Amen.

Scripture:

"I can do all this through him who gives me strength."

– Philippians 4:13

23. Gratitude for Unexpected Blessings

Lord, thank You for the unexpected blessings that come along the way—opportunities, connections, and moments of joy that remind me of Your faithfulness. Help me to see and appreciate these blessings, even when they come in ways I did not expect. Let me approach each day with a heart of gratitude and a spirit of thankfulness for the ways You are working in my life. Amen.

Scripture:

"Every good and perfect gift is from above, coming down from the Father of the heavenly lights, who does not change like shifting shadows."

— James 1:17

24. Cultivating Patience for God's Direction

Father, waiting for Your direction can be difficult, especially when I am eager to know what's next. Help me cultivate patience as I seek Your guidance and trust that You are working in every season. Let me be willing to wait for Your timing and to find contentment in the present while trusting in the future You have planned for me. Amen.

Scripture:

"Wait for the Lord; be strong and take heart and wait for the Lord."

— Psalm 27:14

25. Prayer for Renewed Passion and Purpose

Dear God, as I transition to a new chapter in my career, I pray for a renewed sense of passion and purpose. Let me be excited about the work I do, motivated to make a difference, and filled with a sense of calling to serve others through my career. May my passion reflect Your love, and may my purpose align with Your will for my life. Amen.

Scripture:

"For it is God who works in you to will and to act in order to fulfill his good purpose."

– Philippians 2:13

26. Developing a Flexible Mindset

Lord, help me to be flexible and adaptable as I navigate new environments, challenges, and changes. Let me be open to learning, willing to try new things, and ready to adjust my plans as needed. Teach me to be resilient in the face of uncertainty and let my mindset be one of growth and openness to whatever You have in store for me. Amen.

Scripture:

"Trust in the Lord with all your heart and lean not on your own understanding; in all your ways submit to him, and he will make your paths straight."

– Proverbs 3:5-6

27. Celebrating Every Small Step Forward

Father, help me to celebrate every small step I take in my career transition, knowing that each step is progress. Let me find joy in the journey, appreciate the little victories, and honor the effort it takes to grow and move forward. May my heart be filled with gratitude for every step, and may I continue to strive for greater things in Your name. Amen.

Scripture:

"Rejoice in the Lord always. I will say it again: Rejoice!"

– **Philippians 4:4**

28. Relying on Faith When the Future Feels Unclear

Dear God, there are times when the future feels uncertain, and the path ahead is unclear. Please help me to rely on my faith, to trust that You are leading me even when I don't see the whole picture, and to know that You are working all things for my good. Let my faith be my anchor in moments of doubt, and let me walk in confidence, knowing that You are by my side. Amen.

Scripture:

"Now faith is confidence in what we hope for and assurance about what we do not see."

– **Hebrews 11:1**

29. Confidence in God's Faithfulness in All Transitions

Lord, as I step into a new chapter of my career, help me to have confidence in Your faithfulness. Let me remember the ways You have guided and provided for me in the past, and let me trust that You will continue to be faithful in this new season. May I walk boldly in the assurance that You are with me, leading me to a place of purpose and fulfillment. Amen.

Scripture:

"The Lord is faithful to all his promises and loving toward all he has made."

– **Psalm 145:13**

30. Gratitude for Growth and New Beginnings

Dear God, thank You for this new beginning and the growth that comes with it. I am grateful for the opportunity to start fresh, to learn, to explore, and to move closer to the person You have called me to be. Let me approach this season with an open heart, a willing spirit, and a sense of excitement for all that lies ahead. May my journey be one of continuous growth, learning, and joy. Amen.

Scripture:

"Therefore, if anyone is in Christ, the new creation has come: The old has gone, the new is here!"

— 2 Corinthians 5:17

Action Steps For Each Prayer:

1. Trust in God's Plan for Change

1-Minute Reflection Prompt:

- "What change am I learning to trust God with today?"

1-Minute Scripture Focus: :

- "For I know the plans I have for you, declares the Lord."
  — Jeremiah 29:11

1-Minute Personal Prayer:

- "God, help me trust Your plan in this season of change. Guide me and remind me that You are in control."

Daily Gratitude & Praise Prompt:

- "Today, I trusted God's plan by ____."

Whisper Prayer:

- "Lord, I trust You in this transition."

2. Courage to Embrace New Opportunities

1-Minute Reflection Prompt:

- "What opportunity can I approach with courage today?"

1-Minute Scripture Focus:

- "Be strong and courageous. Do not be afraid." — Joshua 1:9

1-Minute Personal Prayer:

- "God, give me the courage to step into new opportunities with faith, knowing You are with me."

Daily Gratitude & Praise Prompt:

- "Today, I showed courage by ____."

Whisper Prayer:

- "Lord, make me bold."

3. Faith in the Process of Transition

1-Minute Reflection Prompt:

- "Where do I need more faith in this transition?"

1-Minute Scripture Focus:

- "Walk by faith, not by sight." — 2 Corinthians 5:7

1-Minute Personal Prayer:

- "God, strengthen my faith in this season of transition. Help me trust the journey, even when I can't see the full picture."

Daily Gratitude & Praise Prompt:

- "Today, I leaned on faith when ____."

Whisper Prayer:

- "Lord, I trust Your process."

4. Wisdom to Make Sound Decisions

1-Minute Reflection Prompt:

- "What decision requires wisdom today?"

1-Minute Scripture Focus:

- "If any of you lacks wisdom, let him ask of God." — James 1:5

1-Minute Personal Prayer:

- "God, give me wisdom to make choices that honor You and align with Your will for my life."

Daily Gratitude & Praise Prompt:

- "Today, I felt God's wisdom in ____."

Whisper Prayer:

- "Lord, guide my decisions."

5. Gratitude for the Lessons Learned in Past Roles

1-Minute Reflection Prompt:

- "What lesson from a past role am I grateful for today?"

1-Minute Scripture Focus:

- "Give thanks in all circumstances." — 1 Thessalonians 5:18

1-Minute Personal Prayer:

- "God, thank You for the lessons I've learned in my past roles. Help me carry those lessons forward with gratitude."

Daily Gratitude & Praise Prompt:

- "Today, I reflected on the lesson of ____."

Whisper Prayer:

- "Lord, thank You for growth."

6. Patience During Periods of Uncertainty

1-Minute Reflection Prompt:

- "Where do I need patience in this transition?"

1-Minute Scripture Focus:

- "Be still before the Lord and wait patiently for Him." — Psalm 37:7

1-Minute Personal Prayer:

- "God, teach me patience in this season of waiting. Help me trust Your timing and rest in Your promises."

Daily Gratitude & Praise Prompt:

- "Today, I practiced patience by ____."

Whisper Prayer:

- "Lord, give me peace as I wait."

7. Strength to Face Fears of the Unknown

1-Minute Reflection Prompt:

- "What fear do I need to face with strength today?"

1-Minute Scripture Focus:

- "The Lord is my strength and my shield." — Psalm 28:7

1-Minute Personal Prayer:

- "God, give me strength to face the unknown with confidence, knowing You are my protector."

Daily Gratitude & Praise Prompt:

- "Today, I found strength by ____."

Whisper Prayer:

- "Lord, strengthen my heart."

8. Seeking Clarity in New Directions

1-Minute Reflection Prompt:

- "What area of my life needs more clarity today?"

1-Minute Scripture Focus:

- "Your word is a lamp to my feet and a light to my path." — Psalm 119:105

1-Minute Personal Prayer:

- "God, help me see the path You have for me. Illuminate my next steps and give me peace in the journey."

Daily Gratitude & Praise Prompt:

- "Today, I found clarity in ____."

Whisper Prayer:

- "Lord, light my way."

9. Peace Amidst Anxiety Over Changes

1-Minute Reflection Prompt:

- "What change is causing me anxiety, and how can I release it to God today?"

1-Minute Scripture Focus:

- "Cast all your anxiety on Him because He cares for you." — 1 Peter 5:7

1-Minute Personal Prayer:

- "God, calm my anxious thoughts and fill me with Your peace. Help me release my worries to You."

Daily Gratitude & Praise Prompt:

- "Today, I found peace by ____."

Whisper Prayer:

- "Lord, calm my spirit."

10. Grace in Handling Unexpected Detours

1-Minute Reflection Prompt:

- "How can I respond with grace to a detour I'm facing today?"

1-Minute Scripture Focus:

- "My grace is sufficient for you, for my power is made perfect in weakness." — 2 Corinthians 12:9

1-Minute Personal Prayer:

- "God, give me the grace to handle detours and trust that they are part of Your greater plan."

Daily Gratitude & Praise Prompt:

- "Today, I responded with grace by ____."

Whisper Prayer:

- "Lord, help me extend grace."

11. Self-confidence to Try Something New

1-Minute Reflection Prompt:

- "What new opportunity can I approach with confidence today?"

1-Minute Scripture Focus:

- "I can do all things through Christ who strengthens me." — Philippians 4:13

1-Minute Personal Prayer:

- "God, help me embrace new experiences with confidence, knowing You are equipping me for what's ahead."

Daily Gratitude & Praise Prompt:

- "Today, I stepped out in confidence by ____."

Whisper Prayer:

- "Lord, help me believe in myself."

12. Perspective to See Opportunities, Not Setbacks

1-Minute Reflection Prompt:

- "What challenge can I view as an opportunity today?"

1-Minute Scripture Focus:

- "And we know that in all things God works for the good of those who love Him." — Romans 8:28

1-Minute Personal Prayer:

- "God, open my eyes to see Your purpose in every challenge. Help me focus on opportunities instead of setbacks."

Daily Gratitude & Praise Prompt:

- "Today, I found opportunity in ____."

Whisper Prayer:

- "Lord, shift my perspective."

13. Support from Friends and Family During Transitions

1-Minute Reflection Prompt:

- "Who can I lean on or thank for support today?"

1-Minute Scripture Focus:

- "Carry each other's burdens, and in this way, you will fulfill the law of Christ." — Galatians 6:2

1-Minute Personal Prayer:

- "God, thank You for placing supportive people in my life. Help me value and lean on them during this season."

Daily Gratitude & Praise Prompt:

- "Today, I felt supported by ____."

Whisper Prayer:

- "Lord, bless those who support me."

14. Trust in God's Perfect Timing

1-Minute Reflection Prompt:

- "What area of my life do I need to trust God's timing for today?"

1-Minute Scripture Focus:

- "He has made everything beautiful in its time." — Ecclesiastes 3:11

1-Minute Personal Prayer:

- "God, teach me to wait on Your timing and trust that everything is unfolding according to Your plan."

Daily Gratitude & Praise Prompt:

- "Today, I trusted God's timing in ____."

Whisper Prayer:

- "Lord, I surrender to Your timing."

15. Letting Go of What No Longer Serves Them

1-Minute Reflection Prompt:

- "What do I need to release to move forward today?"

1-Minute Scripture Focus:

- "Forget the former things; do not dwell on the past." — Isaiah 43:18

1-Minute Personal Prayer:

- "God, help me let go of what no longer serves me. Make space in my heart for the new things You are doing."

Daily Gratitude & Praise Prompt:

- "Today, I let go of ____ and found freedom."

Whisper Prayer:

- "Lord, help me release the past."

16. Joy in the New Experiences Ahead

1-Minute Reflection Prompt:

- "What new experience can I find joy in today?"

1-Minute Scripture Focus:

- "The joy of the Lord is your strength." — Nehemiah 8:10

1-Minute Personal Prayer:

- "God, fill my heart with joy as I embrace the new experiences You have for me."

Daily Gratitude & Praise Prompt:

- "Today, I found joy in ____."

Whisper Prayer:

- "Lord, fill me with joy."

17. Prayer for Finding the Right Opportunities

1-Minute Reflection Prompt:

- "What opportunity do I need God's guidance to find today?"

1-Minute Scripture Focus:

- "Ask, and it will be given to you; seek, and you will find." — Matthew 7:7

1-Minute Personal Prayer:

- "God, guide me to the right opportunities that align with Your plan for my life. Open doors only. You can open."

Daily Gratitude & Praise Prompt:

- "Today, I sought God's guidance for ____."

Whisper Prayer:

- "Lord, direct my steps."

18. Resilience in Handling Rejections or Delays

1-Minute Reflection Prompt:

- "What rejection or delay can I handle with resilience today?"

1-Minute Scripture Focus:

- "Let us not grow weary of doing good, for at the proper time we will reap a harvest." — Galatians 6:9

1-Minute Personal Prayer:

- "God, strengthen me to face rejection and delays with hope, knowing that You have a plan for me."

Daily Gratitude & Praise Prompt:

- "Today, I grew resilient by ____."

Whisper Prayer:

- "Lord, renew my strength."

19. Seeking a Deeper Purpose in Work

1-Minute Reflection Prompt:

- "How can I find a deeper purpose in my work today?"

1-Minute Scripture Focus:

- "Whatever you do, do it all for the glory of God." — 1 Corinthians 10:31

1-Minute Personal Prayer:

- "God, show me how my work can be a reflection of Your purpose for my life."

Daily Gratitude & Praise Prompt:

- "Today, I felt purpose in ____."

Whisper Prayer:

- "Lord, align my work with Your will."

20. Finding Community and Support in New Roles

1-Minute Reflection Prompt:

- "How can I build community in my current situation?"

1-Minute Scripture Focus:

- "Encourage one another and build each other up." — 1 Thessalonians 5:11

1-Minute Personal Prayer:

- "God, help me connect with others and find support in this new season. Surround me with people who uplift and inspire me."

Daily Gratitude & Praise Prompt:

- "Today, I found community in _____."

Whisper Prayer:

- "Lord, lead me to my people."

21. Overcoming Self-Doubt
1-Minute Reflection Prompt:

- "What self-doubt do I need to overcome today?"

1-Minute Scripture Focus:

- "For the Spirit God gave us does not make us timid, but gives us power, love, and self-discipline." — 2 Timothy 1:7

1-Minute Personal Prayer:

- "God, help me overcome self-doubt. Remind me of the strength and confidence You have placed within me."

Daily Gratitude & Praise Prompt:

- "Today, I overcame self-doubt by _____."

Whisper Prayer:

- "Lord, strengthen my belief in myself."

22. Embracing New Challenges with Faith

1-Minute Reflection Prompt:

- "What challenge can I approach with faith today?"

1-Minute Scripture Focus:

- "I can do all things through Christ who strengthens me." — Philippians 4:13

1-Minute Personal Prayer:

- "God, give me faith to face new challenges head-on. Help me trust that You are equipping me for this moment."

Daily Gratitude & Praise Prompt:

- "Today, I embraced a new challenge by ____."

Whisper Prayer:

- "Lord, help me trust You in the unknown."

23. Gratitude for Unexpected Blessings

1-Minute Reflection Prompt:

- "What unexpected blessing am I grateful for today?"

1-Minute Scripture Focus:

- "Give thanks to the Lord, for He is good; His love endures forever." — Psalm 107:1

1-Minute Personal Prayer:

- "God, thank You for the unexpected blessings in my life. Help me see Your hand in everything, big and small."

Daily Gratitude & Praise Prompt:

- "Today, I felt grateful for ____."

Whisper Prayer:

- "Lord, thank You for Your surprises."

24. Cultivating Patience for God's Direction

1-Minute Reflection Prompt:

- "Where do I need to cultivate patience today?"

1-Minute Scripture Focus:

- "Wait for the Lord; be strong and take heart and wait for the Lord." — Psalm 27:14

1-Minute Personal Prayer:

- "God, teach me to be patient as I seek Your direction. Help me trust that Your timing is always perfect."

Daily Gratitude & Praise Prompt:

- "Today, I practiced patience by ____."

Whisper Prayer:

- "Lord, help me wait with faith."

25. Prayer for Renewed Passion and Purpose

1-Minute Reflection Prompt:

- "What area of my work needs renewed passion or purpose today?"

1-Minute Scripture Focus:

- "Whatever you do, work at it with all your heart, as working for the Lord." — Colossians 3:23

1-Minute Personal Prayer:

- "God, reignite my passion and purpose for the work You've called me to. Help me find joy and fulfillment in it."

Daily Gratitude & Praise Prompt:

- "Today, I felt renewed passion for ____."

Whisper Prayer:

- "Lord, reignite my heart."

26. Developing a Flexible Mindset

1-Minute Reflection Prompt:

- "Where do I need to embrace flexibility today?"

1-Minute Scripture Focus:

- "In their hearts, humans plan their course, but the Lord establishes their steps." — Proverbs 16:9

1-Minute Personal Prayer:

- "God, help me develop a flexible mindset. Teach me to adapt and trust Your redirection in my life."

Daily Gratitude & Praise Prompt:

- "Today, I practiced flexibility by ____."

Whisper Prayer:

- "Lord, shape my thoughts."

27. Celebrating Every Small Step Forward

1-Minute Reflection Prompt:

- "What small step forward can I celebrate today?"

1-Minute Scripture Focus:

- "Do not despise these small beginnings, for the Lord rejoices to see the work begin." — Zechariah 4:10

1-Minute Personal Prayer:

- "God, help me see the value in small progress and celebrate each step toward my goals."

Daily Gratitude & Praise Prompt:

- "Today, I celebrated progress by ____."

Whisper Prayer:

- "Lord, thank You for small victories."

28. Relying on Faith When the Future Feels Unclear

1-Minute Reflection Prompt:

- "What uncertainty can I release to God today?"

1-Minute Scripture Focus:

- "Trust in the Lord with all your heart and lean not on your own understanding." — Proverbs 3:5

1-Minute Personal Prayer:

- "God, help me lean on You when the future feels unclear. Strengthen my faith and remind me You are always in control."

Daily Gratitude & Praise Prompt:

- "Today, I relied on faith by ____."

Whisper Prayer:

- "Lord, I trust You with my future."

29. Confidence in God's Faithfulness in All Transitions

1-Minute Reflection Prompt:

- "Where have I seen God's faithfulness in past transitions?"

1-Minute Scripture Focus:

- "The Lord is faithful to all His promises and loving toward all He has made." — Psalm 145:13

1-Minute Personal Prayer:

- "God, remind me of Your faithfulness in every season of change. Help me trust that You will guide me through this one, too."

Daily Gratitude & Praise Prompt:

- "Today, I felt God's faithfulness when ____."

Whisper Prayer:

- "Lord, thank You for being faithful."

30. Gratitude for Growth and New Beginnings

1-Minute Reflection Prompt:

- "What growth or new beginning can I be thankful for today?"

1-Minute Scripture Focus:

- "See, I am doing a new thing! Now it springs up; do you not perceive it?" — Isaiah 43:19

1-Minute Personal Prayer:

- "God, thank You for the growth and new beginnings You've brought into my life. Help me embrace them with gratitude and hope."

Daily Gratitude & Praise Prompt:

- "Today, I felt grateful for ____."

Whisper Prayer:

- "Lord, thank You for new beginnings."

Chapter Six:
Serving with Heart: Prayers for Helpers, Healers, and Professionals

If you work in healthcare or any service field where you're always helping others, you totally get how tough it can be. It really takes a toll on you mentally, emotionally, and spiritually. It's common to feel stretched thin, juggling tough situations, high demands, and those moments when you just feel exhausted. This collection of prayers is for you—those who dedicate your days to caring for others. It's there to give you support, strength, and hope when you really need it.

There's a prayer that asks for strength to help others out. It recognizes the daily hard work involved in caring for patients and asks God to refresh your compassion, patience, and love, particularly on those days when it feels overwhelming. Feeling tired from compassion fatigue is totally normal, and it's perfectly okay to acknowledge that.

Just keep in mind, it's God's strength that helps you push through when you feel like you're running on empty.

Making tough decisions is just part of what you do. The prayer for wisdom really captures that idea. It's really about seeking the grace and understanding we need to make the right choices when things seem so uncertain. When stress starts to build up, there's a little prayer for peace that can help—it's a nice reminder that God is right there with you, even when everything feels chaotic.

This book is filled with prayers that really connect with those who genuinely care about others, and it also encourages you to take care of yourself. It's important to bring grace, patience, and joy into your work as well. If you're getting through a long shift, handling a challenging patient, or making a tough decision, these prayers can really help you find some spiritual support.

This book aims to offer you peace and inspiration as you navigate the ups and downs of your journey. Every moment you spend helping others shows how much God loves you. Just a little reminder that you're never on your own in what you do.

1. Prayer for Strength in Serving Others

Heavenly Father, as a healthcare professional or service provider, my days are often filled with the needs and concerns of others. Please grant me the strength to serve with compassion, patience, and love. Let me find renewed energy in Your presence, and help me see those I serve. Let my service be a reflection of Your care and grace. Amen.

Scripture:

"The Lord is my strength and my shield; my heart trusts in him, and he helps me. My heart leaps for joy, and with my song, I praise him."

— **Psalm 28:7**

2. Compassion Fatigue—Finding Strength in God

Lord, serving others day in and day out can be physically and emotionally exhausting. There are times when I feel overwhelmed, and my compassion feels like it's running dry. Help me to find strength in You, to be renewed in Your love, and to continue showing care and kindness even when I am weary. Let me remember that my service is an extension of Your love for all people. Amen.

Scripture:

"Come to me, all you who are weary and burdened, and I will give you rest."

— **Matthew 11:28**

3. Gratitude for the Ability to Help and Heal

Father, I am grateful for the opportunity to make a difference in the lives of others through my work. Thank You for giving me the skills, knowledge, and passion to help and heal those who are in need. Let me always remember the privilege it is to serve, and may my work be a reflection of my gratitude for the gifts You have given me. Amen.

Scripture:

"Give thanks to the Lord, for he is good; his love endures forever."

— **Psalm 107:1**

4. Wisdom for Difficult Decisions

Dear God, healthcare professionals or service providers often make difficult decisions that impact the lives and well-being of others. I ask for Your wisdom and guidance as I face these choices. Let me approach each situation with discernment, compassion, and a desire to do what is right and best for those I serve. Help me to lean on Your understanding and trust in Your leading. Amen.

Scripture:

"If any of you lacks wisdom, you should ask God, who gives generously to all without finding fault, and it will be given to you."

– James 1:5

5. Finding Peace Amidst Demanding Work

Lord, my work is often demanding as a healthcare professional, with long hours, high-stress situations, and a constant flow of needs to be met. Help me to find peace amidst the demands, to rest in Your presence, and to approach my work with calm and clarity as this is the demand of this profession. Let me be reminded that You are with me in every moment, giving me strength and peace to carry out my responsibilities. Amen.

Scripture:

"Peace I leave with you; my peace I give you. I do not give to you as the world gives. Do not let your hearts be troubled, and do not be afraid."

– John 14:27

6. Patience with Difficult Patients or Situations

Father, there are times when I encounter difficult patients, challenging situations, or moments that test my patience. Please give me the patience to handle these encounters with grace and understanding. Let me see each person as Your creation, worthy of respect and love, and help me respond with kindness even in the face of frustration. Amen.

Scripture:

"Be completely humble and gentle; be patient, bearing with one another in love."

– Ephesians 4:2

7. Joy in Making a Difference in Others' Lives

Dear God, remind me of the joy that comes from serving others and making a difference in their lives. Help me to find fulfillment in the small victories, the smiles, and the moments when a patient feels heard and cared for. Let me see the impact of my services and find joy in knowing that I am serving as Your hands and feet in the world. Amen.

Scripture:

"The joy of the Lord is your strength."

– Nehemiah 8:10

8. Trust in God's Guidance for Each Day

Lord, every day is different, bringing new challenges, patients, and experiences. Please guide me through each day, helping me to make wise decisions, show compassion, and serve to the best of my ability. Let me trust that You are leading me and that You have a purpose for every interaction and moment. Amen.

Scripture:

"Trust in the Lord with all your heart and lean not on your own understanding; in all your ways submit to him, and he will make your paths straight."

– Proverbs 3:5-6

9. Self-Care for a Well-Rested and Healthy Mind

Dear Father, while my work is about caring for others, I know that I must also take care of myself. Help me to find time for rest, self-care, and moments of rejuvenation. Let me not neglect my own well-being, knowing that a healthy mind and body are essential for serving others effectively. Teach me to balance caring for others with caring for myself. Amen.

Scripture:

"Do you not know that your bodies are temples of the Holy Spirit, who is in you, whom you have received from God? You are not your own."

– 1 Corinthians 6:19

10. Empathy for Patients and Their Families

Dear God, help me to approach every patient and their family with empathy, understanding, and compassion. Let me see beyond their words and actions to the emotions and fears they may be experiencing. Teach me to listen well, to comfort them in their pain, and to provide care that reflects Your love and grace. Amen.

Scripture:

"Rejoice with those who rejoice; mourn with those who mourn."

— **Romans 12:15**

11. Courage to Handle Emergencies or Stress

O Lord, healthcare can be a stressful field, with emergencies and situations that require quick thinking and calmness under pressure. Please give me the courage to face these moments with strength and composure. Let me not be overwhelmed by the stress, but instead find confidence in Your guidance and the skills You have given me. Amen.

Scripture:

"Be strong and courageous. Do not be afraid; do not be discouraged, for the Lord your God will be with you wherever you go."

— **Joshua 1:9**

12. Motivation to Keep Serving Even When Tired

Father, there are times when I feel tired, burnt out, and ready to give up. Please renew my motivation and passion to continue serving others, even when I am weary. Remind me of the impact my work has on the lives of those I care for, and help me to see that every act of service is meaningful and valued. Let me find renewed energy in Your presence. Amen.

Scripture:

"Let us not become weary in doing good, for at the proper time, we will reap a harvest if we do not give up."

— **Galatians 6:9**

13. Balance Between Work and Personal Life

Dear God, help me to find a healthy balance between my work and my personal life. Let me not be consumed by my job to the point of neglecting my family, friends, and own well-being. Teach me to set boundaries, to find joy in my relationships outside of my professional life, and to maintain a balance that allows me to serve well in all areas of my life. Amen.

Scripture:

"The Lord gives strength to his people; the Lord blesses his people with peace."

— **Psalm 29:11**

14. Grace in Responding to Difficult Situations

Lord, in my work, I am often faced with difficult situations, whether it be with patients, colleagues, or circumstances beyond my control. Help me to respond with grace and understanding, to seek peaceful resolutions, and to approach every challenge with a spirit of love and kindness. Let my actions be a reflection of Your grace in my life. Amen.

Scripture:

"Let your conversation be always full of grace, seasoned with salt, so that you may know how to answer everyone."

— **Colossians 4:6**

15. Prayer for Patient Outcomes and Recovery

Dear God, I lift up every patient I serve to You. I pray for their healing, their recovery, and their comfort in times of pain and uncertainty. Please guide me as I care for them, giving me the wisdom to make the right choices and the compassion to support them through their journey. Let Your healing hand be upon every patient, and may they experience Your peace and love. Amen.

Scripture:

"Is anyone among you sick? Let them call the elders of the church to pray over them and anoint them with oil in the name of the Lord."

– James 5:14

16. Clarity in Communicating Effectively

Father, effective communication is essential in my work, whether with patients, their families, or colleagues. Please help me to communicate with clarity, understanding, and empathy. Let my words be helpful, my tone be gentle, and my actions be a reflection of Your love. May every conversation bring comfort, guidance, and support to those I serve. Amen.

Scripture:

"Let your conversation be gracious and attractive so that you will have the right response for everyone."

– Colossians 4:6 (NLT)

17. Encouragement in Feeling Valued and Needed

Lord, there are times when I wonder if my services to mankind truly make a difference, and I struggle to feel valued or appreciated. Please remind me that every act of service, no matter how small, has value in Your eyes. Help me to see the impact of my work and to find encouragement in knowing that I am fulfilling a meaningful purpose by serving others. Amen.

Scripture:

"Whatever you do, work at it with all your heart, as working for the Lord, not for human masters."

– **Colossians** 3:23

18. Support from Colleagues and Peers

Dear God, thank You for the colleagues and peers who work alongside me. I am grateful for their support, encouragement, and friendship. Help us to build a strong team, to lift each other up, and to work together for the good of our patients and our community. Let us be a source of strength to one another and grow together in our shared mission. Amen.

Scripture:

"Two are better than one, because they have a good return for their labor: If either of them falls down, one can help the other up."

– **Ecclesiastes 4:9-10**

19. Rest and Rejuvenation for the Soul

Father, my work is both rewarding and demanding, and there are times when I need rest for my body, mind, and soul. Please help me to find moments of peace and rejuvenation, to take time away from the demands of my job, and to be replenished in Your presence. Let me find true rest in You, knowing that it is okay to pause and be still. Amen.

Scripture:

"He makes me lie down in green pastures, he leads me beside quiet waters, he refreshes my soul."

— Psalm 23:2-3

20. Prayer for Protection Over Health and Safety

Dear Lord, as I serve others, please protect my health and safety. Guard me against illness, injury, and harm as I work in environments that may be challenging or risky. Let Your hand of protection be upon me, and give me the wisdom to take the necessary precautions to stay safe. May I continue to serve others with a spirit of peace and trust in Your protection. Amen.

Scripture:

"The Lord will keep you from all harm—he will watch over your life; the Lord will watch over your coming and going both now and forevermore."

— Psalm 121:7-8

21. Peace Amidst Emotionally Heavy Days

Lord, there are days when the emotional weight of my work feels overwhelming, and the pain and struggles of my patients become heavy on my heart. Please give me peace in these moments, to lay down my burdens before You, and to find comfort in knowing that You are with me. Let me approach every situation with empathy but not be consumed by the emotions that come with it. Amen.

Scripture:

"Cast all your anxiety on him because he cares for you."

— 1 Peter 5:7

22. Developing Resilience in Challenging Situations

Father, as a healthcare professional, often requires resilience—to face tough situations, unexpected challenges, and moments of difficulty. Help me to develop a spirit of resilience, to adapt to challenges with grace, and to keep moving forward even when things are hard. Let me be strong in You, knowing that You are my source of hope and strength. Amen.

Scripture:

"The Lord is my rock, my fortress and my deliverer; my God is my rock, in whom I take refuge."

— Psalm 18:2

23. Building Meaningful Connections with Patients

Dear God, help me to build meaningful and compassionate connections with the patients I serve. Let me see them as individuals with their own stories, struggles, and hopes. Help me to listen well, to show empathy, and to provide care that goes beyond the physical needs. Let my interactions bring comfort, support, and healing. Amen.

Scripture:

"A new command I give you: Love one another. As I have loved you, so you must love one another."

— John 13:34

24. Seeking God's Presence in Every Interaction

Lord, may I seek Your presence in every interaction, every conversation, and every moment of care. Let me approach my work as an opportunity to serve You and to bring Your love to those in need. Help me to see You in each person I meet, and let my work be a reflection of Your grace and compassion. Amen.

Scripture:

"Whatever you did for one of the least of these brothers and sisters of mine, you did for me."

– Matthew 25:40

25. Gratitude for the Privilege to Serve

Father, thank You for the privilege of being able to serve others in my work. Help me to approach each day with a heart of gratitude, knowing that my work has meaning and purpose. Let me never take for granted the opportunity to make a difference in the lives of others, and may I always serve with joy and a spirit of humility. Amen.

Scripture:

"Serve the Lord with gladness; come before his presence with singing."

– Psalm 100:2 (NKJV)

26. Strength to Handle Long Shifts and Workload

Dear God, healthcare often requires long hours, demanding workloads, and the ability to push through exhaustion. Please give me the strength to handle the physical and mental demands of my work. Let me find energy in You, and help me to approach each day with a spirit of perseverance and determination. Amen.

Scripture:

"I can do all this through him who gives me strength."

— **Philippians 4:13**

27. Prayer for Wisdom and Skill in Their Role

Father, I pray for wisdom and skill as I serve in my role as a healthcare professional. Let me use the talents You have given me to bring healing, comfort, and support to those in need. Guide my hands, my mind, and my heart in every task I perform, and may I always seek to serve with excellence and care. Amen.

Scripture:

"Let the wise listen and add to their learning, and let the discerning get guidance."

— **Proverbs 1:5**

28. Trust in God's Hand Over Their Work

Lord, help me to trust that You are guiding every step of my work, every patient I see, and every situation I encounter. Let me not be overwhelmed by the weight of my responsibilities, but instead trust that You are using my hands and heart for Your purposes. May I find comfort in knowing that You are at work in all things. Amen.

Scripture:

"And we know that in all things God works for the good of those who love him, who have been called according to his purpose."

— **Romans 8:28**

29. Overcoming the Fear of Mistakes

Dear God, there are times when I fear making mistakes, knowing that my work has a significant impact on the lives of others. Please help me to overcome this fear and to trust that You are guiding me. Let me approach my work with confidence and carefulness but also with the assurance that Your grace covers my imperfections. Amen.

Scripture:

"For the Spirit God gave us does not make us timid, but gives us power, love and self-discipline."

— **2 Timothy 1:7**

30. Finding Joy in the Journey of Service and Care

Father, let me find joy in the journey of serving others—joy in the moments of healing, in the smiles of patients, and in the connections made along the way. Help me to see every day as an opportunity to make a positive impact and to bring hope to those in need. Let my joy come from knowing that I am fulfilling a greater purpose through my work. Amen.

Scripture:

*"The joy of the Lord is **your** strength."*

— **Nehemiah 8:10**

Action Steps For Each Prayer:

1. Prayer for Strength in Serving Others

1-Minute Reflection Prompt:

- "What task today felt overwhelming, and how can I trust God for renewed strength?"

1-Minute Scripture Focus:

- "The Lord is my strength and my shield; my heart trusts in him, and he helps me. My heart leaps for joy, and with my song I praise him." — Psalm 28:7

1-Minute Personal Prayer:

- "Lord, strengthen me as I serve. Let my heart trust in Your power and reflect Your love."

Daily Gratitude and Praise Prompt:

- "I felt God's strength in my service today when ____."

Whisper Prayer:

- "Lord, be my strength."

2. **Compassion Fatigue—Finding Strength in God**

   1-Minute Reflection Prompt:

   - "Where do I feel most weary, and how can I rely on God for rest?"

   1-Minute Scripture Focus:

   - "Come to me, all you who are weary and burdened, and I will give you rest." — Matthew 11:28

   1-Minute Personal Prayer:

- "Lord, I am weary. Please give me rest and renew my spirit so I can continue to serve with compassion."

Daily Gratitude and Praise Prompt:

- "I found rest in God today when ____."

Whisper Prayer:

- "God, renew my strength."

3. **Gratitude for the Ability to Help and Heal**

    1-Minute Reflection Prompt:

    - "What moment today reminded me of the blessing to help and heal others?"

    1-Minute Scripture Focus:

    - "Give thanks to the Lord, for he is good; his love endures forever." — Psalm 107:1

    1-Minute Personal Prayer:

    - "Lord, thank You for the privilege to serve and the skills You have given me to help others."

    Daily Gratitude and Praise Prompt:

    - "I gave thanks to God for the ability to serve when ____."

    Whisper Prayer:

    - "Thank You, Lord, for letting me help."

4. **Wisdom for Difficult Decisions**

1-Minute Reflection Prompt:

- "What decision today required wisdom, and how did I seek God's guidance?"

1-Minute Scripture Focus:

- "If any of you lacks wisdom, you should ask God, who gives generously to all without finding fault, and it will be given to you." — James 1:5

1-Minute Personal Prayer:

- "Lord, I need Your wisdom to make decisions that honor You and serve others well."

Daily Gratitude and Praise Prompt:

- "I felt God's wisdom in my decisions today when ____."

Whisper Prayer:

- "God, give me wisdom."

5. **Finding Peace Amidst Demanding Work**

   1-Minute Reflection Prompt:

   - "Where did I feel overwhelmed today, and how can I find peace in God's presence?"

   1-Minute Scripture Focus:

   - "Peace, I leave with you; my peace I give you. I do not give to you as the world gives. Do not let your hearts be troubled and do not be afraid." — John 14:27

1-Minute Personal Prayer:

- "Lord, bring peace to my heart and mind amidst the demands of my work."

Daily Gratitude and Praise Prompt:

- "I felt God's peace in my work today when ____."

Whisper Prayer:

- "God, give me peace."

6. **Patience with Difficult Patients or Situations**

    1-Minute Reflection Prompt:

    - "When was my patience tested today, and how did God help me respond with grace?"

    1-Minute Scripture Focus:

    - "Be completely humble and gentle; be patient, bearing with one another in love." — Ephesians 4:2

    1-Minute Personal Prayer:

    - "Lord, help me to show patience and kindness even in the most difficult moments."

    Daily Gratitude and Praise Prompt:

    - "I showed patience today by ____."

    Whisper Prayer:

    - "God, help me be patient."

7. **Joy in Making a Difference in Others' Lives**

   1-Minute Reflection Prompt:

   - "What moment today reminded me of the joy of serving others?"

   1-Minute Scripture Focus:

   - "The joy of the Lord is your strength." — Nehemiah 8:10

   1-Minute Personal Prayer:

   - "Lord, thank You for the joy of serving others and making a difference in their lives."

   Daily Gratitude and Praise Prompt:

   - "I found joy in serving today when ____."

   Whisper Prayer:

   - "Lord, let me serve with joy."

8. **Trust in God's Guidance for Each Day**

   1-Minute Reflection Prompt:

   - "How did I trust God to guide me through the challenges of today?"

   1-Minute Scripture Focus:

   - "Trust in the Lord with all your heart and lean not on your own understanding; in all your ways submit to him, and he will make your paths straight." — Proverbs 3:5-6

   1-Minute Personal Prayer:

- "Lord, guide me in all I do. Help me to trust Your plan for every step I take."

Daily Gratitude and Parise Prompt:

- "I trusted God's guidance today when ____."

Whisper Prayer:

- "Lord, lead me."

9. Self-Care for a Well-Rested and Healthy Mind

1-Minute Reflection Prompt:

- "How did I prioritize self-care today, and how did it impact my service to others?"

1-Minute Scripture Focus:

- "Do you not know that your bodies are temples of the Holy Spirit, who is in you, whom you have received from God? You are not your own." — 1 Corinthians 6:19

1-Minute Personal Prayer:

- "Lord, help me to care for my mind and body as a way to honor You and serve others well."

Daily Gratitude and Parise Prompt:

- "I cared for my well-being today by ____."

Whisper Prayer:

- "Lord, help me rest and recharge."

10. Empathy for Patients and Their Families

1-Minute Reflection Prompt: "How did I show empathy today, and where can I grow in understanding others' needs?"

- **1-Minute Scripture Focus**: "Rejoice with those who rejoice; mourn with those who mourn." — Romans 12:15

- **1-Minute Personal Prayer**: "Lord, help me to approach every interaction with empathy and compassion, reflecting Your love."

- **Gratitude Prompt**: "I showed empathy today by ____."

- **Whisper Prayer**: "God, make me compassionate."

11. Courage to Handle Emergencies or Stress

1-Minute Reflection Prompt:

- "What emergency or stressful situation today required courage, and how did God help me face it?"

1-Minute Scripture Focus:

- "Be strong and courageous. Do not be afraid; do not be discouraged, for the Lord your God will be with you wherever you go." — Joshua 1:9

1-Minute Personal Prayer:

- "Lord, grant me the courage to face emergencies with calmness and strength, trusting in Your presence."

Daily Gratitude and Praise Prompt:

- "I felt God's courage helping me handle stress today when ____."

Whisper Prayer:

- "God, give me courage."

12. Motivation to Keep Serving Even When Tired

1-Minute Reflection Prompt:

- "What moment today reignited my motivation to keep serving despite exhaustion?"

1-Minute Scripture Focus:

- "Let us not become weary in doing good, for at the proper time we will reap a harvest if we do not give up." — Galatians 6:9

1-Minute Personal Prayer:

- "Lord, renew my strength and passion to serve, even when I feel weary. Help me to see the impact of my work."

Daily Gratitude and Praise Prompt:

- "I found renewed motivation today when ____."

Whisper Prayer:

- "God, renew my energy."

13. Balance Between Work and Personal Life

1-Minute Reflection Prompt:

- "What steps did I take today to balance my work and personal life, and how did it help me?"

1-Minute Scripture Focus:

- "The Lord gives strength to his people; the Lord blesses his people with peace." — Psalm 29:11

1-Minute Personal Prayer:

- "Lord, teach me to set boundaries and find peace in balancing my work and personal life."

Daily Gratitude and Praise Prompt:

- "I felt God's peace in balancing my day when _____."

Whisper Prayer:

- "Lord, bring balance to my life."

14. Grace in Responding to Difficult Situations

1-Minute Reflection Prompt:

- "What difficult situation did I face today, and how can I respond with more grace tomorrow?"

1-Minute Scripture Focus:

- "Let your conversation be always full of grace, seasoned with salt, so that you may know how to answer everyone." — Colossians 4:6

1-Minute Personal Prayer:

- "Lord, help me to respond to challenges with grace, understanding, and kindness."

Daily Gratitude and Praise Prompt:

- "I felt God's grace in responding to challenges today when ___."

Whisper Prayer:

- "God, fill me with grace."

15. Prayer for Patient Outcomes and Recovery

1-Minute Reflection Prompt:

- "Which patient today can I lift up in prayer for their healing and recovery?"

1-Minute Scripture Focus:

- "Is anyone among you sick? Let them call the elders of the church to pray over them and anoint them with oil in the name of the Lord." — James 5:14

1-Minute Personal Prayer:

- "Lord, I lift up my patients to You. Guide their healing process and comfort them in their pain."

Daily Gratitude and Praise Prompt:

- "I saw God's hand in a patient's recovery today when ___."

Whisper Prayer:

- "Lord, heal them."

16. Clarity in Communicating Effectively

1-Minute Reflection Prompt:

- "What conversation today needed more clarity, and how can I improve tomorrow?"

1-Minute Scripture Focus:

- "Let your conversation be gracious and attractive so that you will have the right response for everyone." — Colossians 4:6 (NLT)

1-Minute Personal Prayer:

- "Lord, guide my words to be clear, compassionate, and full of understanding in every conversation."

Daily Gratitude and Praise Prompt:

- "I communicated effectively today when _____."

Whisper Prayer:

- "God, guide my words."

17. Encouragement in Feeling Valued and Needed

1-Minute Reflection Prompt:

- "What moment today reminded me that my work has value in God's eyes?"

1-Minute Scripture Focus:

- "Whatever you do, work at it with all your heart, as working for the Lord, not for human masters." — Colossians 3:23

1-Minute Personal Prayer:

- "Lord, remind me that my service matters, and let me find encouragement in fulfilling my purpose."

Daily Gratitude and Praise Prompt:

- "I felt valued in my work today when ____."

Whisper Prayer:

- "Lord, remind me of my worth."

18. Support from Colleagues and Peers

1-Minute Reflection Prompt:

- "How did a colleague or peer support me today, and how can I return the favor?"

1-Minute Scripture Focus:

- "Two are better than one, because they have a good return for their labor: If either of them falls down, one can help the other up." — Ecclesiastes 4:9-10

1-Minute Personal Prayer:

- "Lord, thank You for the colleagues and peers You've placed in my life. Help us to work together in unity."

Daily Gratitude and Praise Prompt:

- "I felt supported by my team today when ____."

Whisper Prayer:

- "God, bless our teamwork."

19. Rest and Rejuvenation for the Soul

1-Minute Reflection Prompt:

- "What moments of rest did I find today, and how can I embrace them more fully?"

1-Minute Scripture Focus:

- "He makes me lie down in green pastures, he leads me beside quiet waters, he refreshes my soul." — Psalm 23:2-3

1-Minute Personal Prayer:

- "Lord, help me find rest in You and rejuvenation for my body, mind, and spirit."

Daily Gratitude and Praise Prompt:

- "I felt God's refreshing presence today when ____."

Whisper Prayer:

- "Lord, refresh my soul."

20. Prayer for Protection Over Health and Safety

1-Minute Reflection Prompt:

- "Where did I see God's protection in my work today, and how can I continue to trust Him?"

1-Minute Scripture Focus:

- "The Lord will keep you from all harm—he will watch over your life; the Lord will watch over your coming and going both now and forevermore." — Psalm 121:7-8

1-Minute Personal Prayer:

- "Lord, protect my health and safety as I serve others. Let me trust in Your care."

Daily Gratitude and Praise Prompt:

- "I felt God's protection over me today when ____."

Whisper Prayer:

- "God, keep me safe."

21. Peace Amidst Emotionally Heavy Days

1-Minute Reflection Prompt:

- "What emotional burden am I carrying today, and how can I cast it onto God?"

1-Minute Scripture Focus:

- "Cast all your anxiety on him because he cares for you." — 1 Peter 5:7

1-Minute Personal Prayer:

- "Lord, help me find peace amidst the emotional weight of my work by laying my burdens before You."

Daily Gratitude and Praise Prompt:

- "I found peace in God's care today when ____."

Whisper Prayer:

- "God, bring me peace."

22. Developing Resilience in Challenging Situations

1-Minute Reflection Prompt:

- "What challenge tested my resilience today, and how did I rely on God for strength?"

1-Minute Scripture Focus:

- "The Lord is my rock, my fortress and my deliverer; my God is my rock, in whom I take refuge." — Psalm 18:2

1-Minute Personal Prayer:

- "Lord, strengthen my resilience and help me face challenges with courage and grace."

Daily Gratitude and Praise Prompt:

- "I found resilience in God's presence today when ____."

Whisper Prayer:

- "Lord, be my rock."

23. Building Meaningful Connections with Patients

1-Minute Reflection Prompt:

- "What moment today helped me connect with a patient on a deeper level?"

1-Minute Scripture Focus:

- "A new command I give you: Love one another. As I have loved you, so you must love one another." — John 13:34

1-Minute Personal Prayer:

- "Lord, guide me to build meaningful connections with my patients and reflect Your love in every interaction."

Daily Gratitude and Praise Prompt:

- "I built a meaningful connection today when ____."

Whisper Prayer:

- "God, help me love as You love."

24. Seeking God's Presence in Every Interaction

1-Minute Reflection Prompt:

- "How did I seek God's presence in my work today?"

1-Minute Scripture Focus:

- "Whatever you did for one of the least of these brothers and sisters of mine, you did for me." — Matthew 25:40

1-Minute Personal Prayer:

- "Lord, let Your presence guide every interaction I have, bringing comfort and grace to others."

Daily Gratitude and Praise Prompt:

- "I felt God's presence in my work today when ____."

Whisper Prayer:

- "God, let me see You in others."

25. Gratitude for the Privilege to Serve

1-Minute Reflection Prompt:

- "What moment today reminded me of the privilege of serving others?"

1-Minute Scripture Focus:

- "Serve the Lord with gladness; come before his presence with singing." — Psalm 100:2 (NKJV)

1-Minute Personal Prayer:

- "Lord, thank You for the privilege of serving others. Let my work always reflect a heart of gratitude."

Daily Gratitude and Praise Prompt:

- "I was grateful for the opportunity to serve today when ____."

Whisper Prayer:

- "Thank You, Lord, for letting me serve."

26. Strength to Handle Long Shifts and Workload

1-Minute Reflection Prompt:

- "What challenge today tested my endurance, and how did I draw strength from God?"

1-Minute Scripture Focus:

- "I can do all this through him who gives me strength." — Philippians 4:13

1-Minute Personal Prayer:

- "Lord, give me the strength to endure long hours and demanding tasks with perseverance."

Daily Gratitude and Praise Prompt:

- "I felt God's strength helping me persevere today when _____."

Whisper Prayer:

- "God, strengthen me."

27. Prayer for Wisdom and Skill in Their Role

1-Minute Reflection Prompt:

- "What situation today required wisdom, and how did I seek God's guidance?"

1-Minute Scripture Focus:

- "Let the wise listen and add to their learning, and let the discerning get guidance." — Proverbs 1:5

1-Minute Personal Prayer:

- "Lord, guide my hands, mind, and heart as I serve, and help me to grow in wisdom and skill."

Daily Gratitude and Praise Prompt:

- "I felt God's wisdom in my work today when _____."

Whisper Prayer:

- "God, grant me wisdom."

28. Trust in God's Hand Over Their Work

1-Minute Reflection Prompt:

- "What moment today reminded me to trust that God is in control of my work?"

1-Minute Scripture Focus:

- "And we know that in all things God works for the good of those who love him, who have been called according to his purpose." — Romans 8:28

1-Minute Personal Prayer:

- "Lord, help me trust that You are guiding my work for a greater purpose."

Daily Gratitude and Praise Prompt:

- "I trusted God's hand in my work today when _____."

Whisper Prayer:

- "Lord, I trust You."

29. Overcoming the Fear of Mistakes

1-Minute Reflection Prompt:

- "What fear held me back today, and how did I trust God to guide me through it?"

1-Minute Scripture Focus:

- "For the Spirit God gave us does not make us timid, but gives us power, love and self-discipline." — 2 Timothy 1:7

1-Minute Personal Prayer:

"Lord, help me to release the fear of mistakes and trust in Your guidance and grace."

Daily Gratitude and Praise Prompt:

- "I overcame fear today by trusting God when ____."

Whisper Prayer:

- "God, guide my steps."

30. Finding Joy in the Journey of Service and Care

1-Minute Reflection Prompt:

- "What moment today brought me joy in serving others?"

1-Minute Scripture Focus:

- "The joy of the Lord is your strength." — Nehemiah 8:10

1-Minute Personal Prayer:

- "Lord, thank You for the joy of serving others. Help me to see each moment as a reflection of Your purpose."

Daily Gratitude and Praise Prompt:

- "I found joy in my service today when ____."

Whisper Prayer:

- "Lord, fill me with joy."

Chapter Seven:
Navigating Relationships Beyond Family

Relationships are the foundation of human experience, shaping who we are and how we interact with the world around us. Yet, maintaining meaningful connections can be one of life's greatest challenges. Whether in friendships, family, workplaces, or communities, relationships often test our patience, compassion, and resilience. *Prayers and Action Steps* serve as a guide to navigating these complexities with faith and purpose, blending spiritual reflection with tangible steps to strengthen and heal relationships.

This chapter is rooted in the belief that prayer is both a sanctuary and a catalyst for transformation. It emphasizes that while prayer opens our hearts to God's guidance, true change requires us to act intentionally in our interactions. Each section provides a focused prayer followed by practical steps that encourage readers to engage with others in love and humility. From resolving conflicts to building lasting friendships, the chapter offers tools to address a variety of relational challenges.

Sections like "Healing the Hurt," "Building Bridges," and "Grace in Conflict" delve into the realities of strained relationships, offering a path toward forgiveness, understanding, and reconciliation. These prayers are not only about seeking divine intervention but also about aligning our hearts and actions with God's purpose. By doing so, we can approach even the most difficult relationships with empathy and hope.

Prayers and Action Steps also emphasize the proactive nature of relationships—celebrating moments of joy, encouraging others, and fostering unity. Whether through small acts of kindness or significant efforts to mend broken connections, the chapter reminds us that every action, no matter how small, has the potential to reflect God's love and strengthen the bonds we share.

This chapter invites readers to step into their relationships with a renewed sense of purpose. It challenges us to see relationships as opportunities for growth, not just through the ease of harmony but through the lessons learned in struggle and repair. By coupling prayer with actionable steps, this chapter provides a framework for living out God's call to love and serve others in every sphere of life.

In *Prayers and Action Steps*, you will find the tools to nurture, heal, and elevate your relationships. It is a reminder that while relationships may be complex and, at times, painful, they are also sacred spaces where God's grace can be most powerfully revealed. Through faith, intention, and perseverance, this chapter equips readers to cultivate connections that honor both God and the people He has placed in their lives.

1. Strengthening Bonds: Prayers for Lasting Friendships

Dear Lord, thank You for the gift of friendship and the people You've placed in my life. Help me to nurture these relationships with love, patience, and kindness. Teach me to be a better friend—one who listens, supports, and uplifts. Let my actions reflect Your love, building strong, lasting bonds that glorify You. May our friendships bring joy, encouragement, and a shared faith that strengthens us both. Amen.

Scripture:

"A friend loves at all times, and a brother is born for a time of adversity."

– Proverbs 17:17

2. Grace in Conflict: Prayers for Resolving Disagreements

Lord, disagreements can strain even the strongest relationships. Please grant me the wisdom to approach conflicts with grace and humility. Help me to listen without judgment, respond with kindness, and seek resolution that honors You. Let Your peace guide my heart and words, bringing understanding and healing to every conversation. Amen.

Scripture:

"Do not let the sun go down while you are still angry."

– Ephesians 4:26

3. Leading with Love: Prayers for Workplace Relationships

Heavenly Father, thank You for the opportunity to work alongside others. Teach me to lead with love, integrity, and respect. Help me to see my coworkers as You see them and to foster an environment of collaboration and kindness. May my actions reflect Your light, inspiring trust and unity in our workplace. Amen.

Scripture:

> *"Do to others as you would have them do to you."*
>
> **– Luke 6:31**

4. A Heart for Community: Prayers for Serving Others

Lord, give me a heart for serving others in my community. Help me to see the needs around me and respond with compassion and generosity. May my actions reflect Your love, bringing hope and encouragement to those I encounter. Let my service be a light that points others to You. Amen.

Scripture:

> *"Each of you should use whatever gift you have received to serve others, as faithful stewards of God's grace in its various forms."*
>
> **– 1 Peter 4:10**

5. Building Bridges: Prayers for Healing Broken Connections

God, You are the ultimate healer of broken relationships. I bring before You the connections in my life that are strained or damaged. Soften my heart and the hearts of those involved. Help us to seek forgiveness and understanding, building a bridge of reconciliation that reflects Your grace. Amen.

Scripture:

"Bear with each other and forgive one another if any of you has a grievance against someone. Forgive as the Lord forgave you."

– Colossians 3:13

6. Finding Your People: Prayers for Meaningful Friendships

Dear God, I long for meaningful friendships that bring encouragement, joy, and mutual growth. Guide me to the people You've prepared to walk alongside me in this journey. Help me to be open, authentic, and loving, creating space for true connection. Thank You for Your faithfulness in providing relationships that reflect Your love. Amen.

Scripture:

"Two are better than one because they have a good return for their labor: If either of them falls down, one can help the other up."

– Ecclesiastes 4:9-10

7. Love Thy Neighbor: Prayers for Community Engagement

Lord, help me to love my neighbors as You command. Show me how to be an active, caring presence in my community. Let me build connections that uplift and inspire, and may my actions be a testimony of Your love and grace. Teach me to serve with humility and joy, reflecting Your heart in all I do. Amen.

Scripture:

"Love your neighbor as yourself."

— Matthew 22:39

8. Navigating Challenges: Prayers for Difficult Relationships

Father, some relationships in my life are challenging. Give me the strength to navigate these with patience, wisdom, and love. Help me to respond to hurt with kindness and to set healthy boundaries when needed. Let Your peace guide my interactions, and may Your love transform our struggles into growth. Amen.

Scripture:

"If it is possible, as far as it depends on you, live at peace with everyone."

— Romans 12:18

9. New Beginnings: Prayers for Forming Fresh Connections

God, stepping into new relationships can feel uncertain, but I trust You to guide me. Help me to approach new connections with openness and sincerity. Let Your Spirit lead me to people who will enrich my journey and bring mutual encouragement. Thank You for the blessings that come with new beginnings. Amen.

Scripture:

"Forget the former things; do not dwell on the past. See, I am doing a new thing!"

– Isaiah 43:18-19

10. Walking in Forgiveness: Prayers for Reconciliation

Lord, forgiveness is not always easy, but I know it's what You call me to do. Help me to release bitterness and embrace forgiveness, just as You have forgiven me. Bring reconciliation where it's possible and healing where it's not. Let my heart reflect Your mercy and grace in every relationship. Amen.

Scripture:

"Be kind and compassionate to one another, forgiving each other, just as in Christ God forgave you."

– Ephesians 4:32

11. The Power of Kindness: Prayers for Everyday Encounters

Lord, help me to reflect Your kindness in all my daily interactions. Teach me to see the value in every person I meet and to respond with love and compassion. May my words and actions bring encouragement, hope, and joy, even in the smallest moments. Let my kindness point others to You. Amen.

Scripture:

"Be kind and compassionate to one another, forgiving each other, just as in Christ God forgave you."

– Ephesians 4:32

12. Lifting Each Other Up: Prayers for Encouraging Friends

Dear God, thank You for the friends You've placed in my life. Show me how to be a source of encouragement, lifting them up with my words and actions. Help me to celebrate their victories, support them in their struggles, and remind them of Your faithfulness. May our friendship be a reflection of Your love. Amen.

Scripture:

"Therefore encourage one another and build each other up, just as in fact you are doing."

– 1 Thessalonians 5:11

13. Harmony at Work: Prayers for Healthy Professional Dynamics

Lord, I thank You for the team I work with. Help us to work together in unity, valuing each other's contributions and respecting one another. May our collaboration be marked by patience, understanding, and a shared purpose. Let Your peace and wisdom guide our professional relationships. Amen.

Scripture:

"How good and pleasant it is when God's people live together in unity!"

– Psalm 133:1

14. Embracing Diversity: Prayers for Understanding Differences

God, You have created each of us uniquely, and I thank You for the beauty in diversity. Help me to approach differences with curiosity and respect, seeking to understand rather than judge. Teach me to love as You love, celebrating the richness of our unique perspectives and experiences. Amen.

Scripture:

"There is neither Jew nor Gentile, neither slave nor free, nor is there male and female, for you are all one in Christ Jesus."

– Galatians 3:28

15. Rooted in Love: Prayers for Deepening Connections

Father, I want my relationships to be rooted in love. Teach me to nurture my connections with patience, honesty, and grace. Let my relationships be grounded in mutual respect and understanding, and may they grow stronger as we reflect Your love to one another. Amen.

Scripture:

"Let all that you do be done in love."

– 1 Corinthians 16:14

16. Stepping Out in Faith: Prayers for Meeting New People

Lord, meeting new people can feel daunting, but I trust You to guide me. Give me the courage to step out of my comfort zone and build meaningful connections. Help me to approach new relationships with openness and sincerity, trusting that You are bringing the right people into my life. Amen.

Scripture:

"For we live by faith, not by sight."

– 2 Corinthians 5:7

17. A Helping Hand: Prayers for Supporting Others in Need

Dear God, show me how to be a source of help and hope to those in need. Open my eyes to see the opportunities to serve others and give me the strength and willingness to act. Let my actions reflect Your love and compassion, and may I bring comfort and encouragement wherever I go. Amen.

Scripture:

"Carry each other's burdens, and in this way, you will fulfill the law of Christ."

– Galatians 6:2

18. Healing the Hurt: Prayers for Letting Go of Resentment

Lord, holding onto resentment weighs heavy on my heart. Help me to release the pain and forgive, as You have forgiven me. Heal the wounds of my past and restore peace to my spirit. Let Your grace flow through me, bringing healing to broken places in my life and relationships. Amen.

Scripture:

"Get rid of all bitterness, rage and anger, brawling and slander, along with every form of malice."

– Ephesians 4:31

19. Celebrating Together: Prayers for Joyful Relationships

God, thank You for the joy that comes from shared moments with loved ones. Help me to celebrate with others in both big and small ways. Let my relationships be filled with laughter, gratitude, and love, bringing glory to You in our shared joy. Amen.

Scripture:

"Rejoice with those who rejoice; mourn with those who mourn."

– Romans 12:15

20. God at the Center: Prayers for Spirit-Led Connections

Lord, I invite You to be the foundation of my relationships. Help me to keep You at the center, guiding my words and actions with Your Spirit. Let my connections be marked by love, patience, and grace, reflecting Your presence in all I do. Amen.

Scripture:

"Above all, love each other deeply, because love covers over a multitude of sins."

– 1 Peter 4:8

21. Patience in Differences: Prayers for Understanding Others

Lord, help me to be patient when I encounter differences in opinions, beliefs, or actions. Teach me to listen with an open heart and seek to understand rather than judge. May Your love guide me in building connections that honor You, even when we don't see eye to eye. Let patience and grace be the foundation of my relationships. Amen.

Scripture:

"Be completely humble and gentle; be patient, bearing with one another in love."

– Ephesians 4:2

22. Boundaries with Grace: Prayers for Protecting Healthy Relationships

God, help me to establish and respect healthy boundaries in my relationships. Give me the wisdom to discern when to say "yes" and the courage to say "no" with love. Let my boundaries be a reflection of Your care for my well-being, protecting my peace while nurturing mutual respect. Amen.

Scripture:

"Above all else, guard your heart, for everything you do flows from it."

– Proverbs 4:23

23. Joy in Togetherness: Prayers for Strengthening Community Bonds

Lord, thank You for the joy of being part of a community. Help me to cherish the togetherness we share, celebrating the blessings of unity and mutual support. May our time together be filled with laughter, love, and encouragement, reflecting the joy that comes from being Your people. Amen.

Scripture:

"How good and pleasant it is when God's people live together in unity!"

– Psalm 133:1

24. Speaking Life: Prayers for Words That Build Up

Dear Lord, help me to choose my words carefully so that they bring life and encouragement to others. Let my speech reflect kindness, truth, and grace, uplifting those around me. May my words be a reflection of Your love, building bridges of connection and inspiring hope. Amen.

Scripture:

"Gracious words are a honeycomb, sweet to the soul and healing to the bones."

– Proverbs 16:24

25. Overcoming Loneliness: Prayers for Finding Connection

Lord, loneliness can feel overwhelming at times. Please remind me that I am never truly alone because You are always with me. Lead me to connections that bring joy, encouragement, and companionship. Help me to step out in faith and seek the community You've prepared for me. Amen.

Scripture:

"The Lord is close to the brokenhearted and saves those who are crushed in spirit."

– Psalm 34:18

26. Gratitude for Friendship: Prayers for Cherishing Those Close to You

Heavenly Father, thank You for the gift of friendship. I am so grateful for the people who bring joy, comfort, and encouragement into my life. Help me to show my appreciation for them and nurture these relationships with love and care. May I never take these blessings for granted. Amen.

Scripture:

"Greater love has no one than this: to lay down one's life for one's friends."

– John 15:13

27. Support in Trials: Prayers for Being There for Others

God, show me how to be a source of strength and support for those going through trials. Give me the words to comfort, the wisdom to listen, and the love to stand by them in their struggles. Let me reflect on Your presence in their lives, reminding them they are never alone. Amen.

Scripture:

"Carry each other's burdens, and in this way, you will fulfill the law of Christ."

– Galatians 6:2

28. Unity in Diversity: Prayers for Bridging Cultural Gaps

Lord, thank You for the diversity You have created in the world. Help me to see the beauty in our differences and work toward understanding and unity. Let Your love guide me in building bridges that bring people together and glorify You in every interaction. Amen.

Scripture:

"Make every effort to keep the unity of the Spirit through the bond of peace."

— **Ephesians 4:3**

29. Hope for Restoration: Prayers for Rekindling Lost Relationships

Father, I bring before You the relationships in my life that have been broken or lost. If it is Your will, help me to rekindle these connections with forgiveness, grace, and hope. Guide my heart and theirs toward reconciliation and healing. Let Your love mend what has been torn. Amen.

Scripture:

"He restores my soul; He leads me in paths of righteousness for His name's sake."

— **Psalm 23:3**

30. Trust in God's Timing: Prayers for Waiting on the Right Connections

Lord, I trust Your timing in bringing the right people into my life. Teach me to be patient and to find peace in the waiting. Help me to recognize the relationships You are orchestrating for my good, and let me walk in faith, knowing You are always working in my favor. Amen.

Scripture:

"There is a time for everything, and a season for every activity under the heavens."

— **Ecclesiastes 3:1**

Action Steps for Each Prayer:

1. Strengthening Bonds: Prayers for Lasting Friendships

1-Minute Reflection Prompt:
- What is one way God has blessed me through a friendship today?

1-Minute Scripture Focus:
- "A friend loves at all times, and a brother is born for a time of adversity." – Proverbs 17:17

Reflect on how God has used your friends to bring encouragement and support.

1-Minute Personal Prayer:
- God, thank You for the friends You've placed in my life. Help me to cherish and nurture these relationships. Teach me to be a source of love, encouragement, and patience, and remind me that friendship is a gift from You. Amen.

Daily Gratitude & Praise Prompt:
- "I showed gratitude for my friendships today by ____."

Whisper Prayer:
- "Thank You for the friends who uplift me."

2. Grace in Conflict: Prayers for Resolving Disagreements

1-Minute Reflection Prompt:
- What is one relationship where I need God's help to bring peace today?

1-Minute Scripture Focus:
- "Do not let the sun go down while you are still angry." – Ephesians 4:26

Reflect on how God's grace can guide you to approach disagreements with humility and love.

1-Minute Personal Prayer:
- Lord, thank You for the opportunity to seek peace in relationships. Help me approach conflicts with grace, wisdom, and patience. Remind me that resolving disagreements honors You. Amen.

Daily Gratitude & Praise Prompt:
- "I demonstrated grace in a disagreement today by ____."

Whisper Prayer:
- "Thank You for Your peace in my relationships."

3. Leading with Love: Prayers for Workplace Relationships

1-Minute Reflection Prompt:
- What is one way God has given me the opportunity to lead with love at work today?

1-Minute Scripture Focus:
- "Do to others as you would have them do to you." – Luke 6:31

Reflect on how God calls you to model respect and integrity in your work relationships.

1-Minute Personal Prayer:
- God, thank You for the ability to influence others positively at work. Help me lead with love, integrity, and kindness, and remind me that my actions can reflect Your light. Amen.

Daily Gratitude & Praise Prompt:
- "I created a positive environment at work today by ____."

Whisper Prayer:
- "Thank You for my work and my coworkers."

4. A Heart for Community: Prayers for Serving Others

1-Minute Reflection Prompt:
- What is one way God has called me to serve my community today?

1-Minute Scripture Focus:
- "And God is able to bless you abundantly..." – 2 Corinthians 9:8

Reflect on how God has equipped you to give back with compassion and love.

1-Minute Personal Prayer:
- Lord, thank You for the opportunity to serve others. I was hoping you could help me recognize the needs around me and respond with generosity and joy. Remind me that serving others is a way to honor You. Amen.

Daily Gratitude & Praise Prompt:
- "I brought hope to someone today by ____."

Whisper Prayer:
- "Thank You for the opportunity to make a difference."

5. Building Bridges: Prayers for Healing Broken Connections

1-Minute Reflection Prompt:
- What relationship in my life needs healing that I can trust God to mend?

1-Minute Scripture Focus:
- "Bear with each other and forgive one another if any of you has a grievance against someone." – Colossians 3:13

Reflect on how God's forgiveness inspires you to rebuild bridges of connection.

1-Minute Personal Prayer:
- God, thank You for being the ultimate healer of relationships. Help me extend grace and forgiveness to those I am estranged from. Teach me to seek reconciliation and honor You in the process. Amen.

Daily Gratitude & Praise Prompt:
- "I worked toward healing a relationship today by ____."

Whisper Prayer:
- "Thank You for the gift of reconciliation."

6. Finding Your People: Prayers for Meaningful Friendships

1-Minute Reflection Prompt:
- Who is one person I can connect with to grow a meaningful friendship?

1-Minute Scripture Focus:
- "And God is able to bless you abundantly..." – 2 Corinthians 9:8

Reflect on how God provides opportunities for meaningful relationships in your life.

1-Minute Personal Prayer:
- God, thank You for the gift of new connections. Guide me to people who will bring joy, encouragement, and mutual growth. Help me approach friendships with authenticity and love. Amen.

Daily Gratitude & Praise Prompt:
- "I nurtured a meaningful connection today by ____."

Whisper Prayer:
- "Thank You for bringing people into my life."

7. Love Thy Neighbor: Prayers for Community Engagement

1-Minute Reflection Prompt:
- What is one way I can show love and kindness to someone in my community today?

1-Minute Scripture Focus:
- "Love your neighbor as yourself." – Matthew 22:39

Reflect on how God calls you to be a light in your community through acts of kindness.

1-Minute Personal Prayer:
- God, thank You for the chance to love and serve my neighbors. Help me to build connections that bring joy and hope to others, reflecting Your love in all I do. Amen.

Daily Gratitude & Praise Prompt:
- "I engaged with my community today by ____."

Whisper Prayer:
- "Thank You for the people in my community."

8. Navigating Challenges: Prayers for Difficult Relationships

1-Minute Reflection Prompt:
- What is one relationship where I can ask God to help me show patience and love?

1-Minute Scripture Focus:
- "If it is possible, as far as it depends on you, live at peace with everyone." – Romans 12:18

Reflect on how God calls you to approach challenging relationships with love and peace.

1-Minute Personal Prayer:
- God, thank You for Your example of love and grace. Help me to show patience and understanding in difficult relationships and to rely on You for strength. Amen.

Daily Gratitude & Praise Prompt:
- "I managed a challenging relationship today by _____."

Whisper Prayer:
- "Thank You for Your peace in my heart."

9. New Beginnings: Prayers for Forming Fresh Connections

1-Minute Reflection Prompt:
- What is one new relationship where I can ask God to guide my heart and actions?

1-Minute Scripture Focus:
- "Forget the former things; do not dwell on the past. See, I am doing a new thing!" – Isaiah 43:18-19

Reflect on how God creates opportunities for new connections and beginnings.

1-Minute Personal Prayer:
- God, thank You for the blessing of new beginnings. Help me to approach fresh connections with trust and sincerity, knowing that You are guiding me. Amen.

Daily Gratitude & Praise Prompt:
- "I embraced new beginnings today by ____."

Whisper Prayer:
- "Thank You for new opportunities to connect."

10. Walking in Forgiveness: Prayers for Reconciliation

1-Minute Reflection Prompt:
- Who is one person I need to forgive or seek reconciliation with today?

1-Minute Scripture Focus:
- "Be kind and compassionate to one another, forgiving each other, just as in Christ God forgave you." – Ephesians 4:32

Reflect on how God's forgiveness empowers you to forgive others.

1-Minute Personal Prayer:
- Lord, thank You for forgiving me. Help me to release bitterness and extend grace to others, seeking reconciliation and peace where it is possible. Amen.

Daily Gratitude & Praise Prompt:
- "I worked toward reconciliation today by ____."

Whisper Prayer:
- "Thank You for teaching me to forgive."

11. The Power of Kindness: Prayers for Everyday Encounters

1-Minute Reflection Prompt:
- What is one interaction today where I showed or could have shown kindness?

1-Minute Scripture Focus:
- "Be kind and compassionate to one another, forgiving each other, just as in Christ God forgave you." – Ephesians 4:32

Reflect on how kindness reflects God's heart to the world.

1-Minute Personal Prayer:
- Lord, thank You for the opportunities to show kindness today. Help me reflect Your love in every interaction, even in the smallest moments. Teach me to see the value in each person I meet and respond with compassion and grace. Amen.

Daily Gratitude & Praise Prompt:
- "I showed kindness today by ____."

Whisper Prayer:
- "Help me spread kindness today."

12. Lifting Each Other Up: Prayers for Encouraging Friends

1-Minute Reflection Prompt:
- What is one way I can encourage a friend today?

1-Minute Scripture Focus:
- "Therefore encourage one another and build each other up, just as in fact you are doing." – 1 Thessalonians 5:11

Reflect on the power of words and actions to uplift others.

1-Minute Personal Prayer:
- Dear God, thank You for the friends who bring joy and encouragement into my life. Show me how to lift them up with my words and actions, celebrating their victories and supporting them in their struggles. May our friendships reflect Your love. Amen.

Daily Gratitude & Praise Prompt:
- "I encouraged someone today by ____."

Whisper Prayer:
- "Thank You for friends who inspire me."

13. Harmony at Work: Prayers for Healthy Professional Dynamics

1-Minute Reflection Prompt:
- What is one way I can promote unity and respect in my workplace today?

1-Minute Scripture Focus:
- "How good and pleasant it is when God's people live together in unity!" – Psalm 133:1

Reflect on how collaboration and harmony glorify God.

1-Minute Personal Prayer:
- Lord, thank You for my coworkers and the team I am part of. Help us to work together in unity, valuing each other's contributions. Guide our interactions with patience and understanding, and let Your wisdom bring peace to our workplace. Amen.

Daily Gratitude & Praise Prompt:
- "I brought harmony to my workplace today by ____."

Whisper Prayer:
- "Bless my workplace with harmony."

14. Embracing Diversity: Prayers for Understanding Differences

1-Minute Reflection Prompt:
- What is one way I can better understand and celebrate the differences in others today?

1-Minute Scripture Focus:
- "There is neither Jew nor Gentile, neither slave nor free, nor is there male and female, for you are all one in Christ Jesus." – Galatians 3:28

Reflect on how diversity is part of God's design.

1-Minute Personal Prayer:
- God, thank You for creating each of us uniquely. Teach me to approach differences with curiosity and respect, seeking to understand rather than judge. Help me celebrate the beauty in diversity, reflecting Your love in every interaction. Amen.

Daily Gratitude & Praise Prompt:
- "I embraced diversity today by ____."

Whisper Prayer:
- "Help me embrace differences with love."

15. Rooted in Love: Prayers for Deepening Connections

1-Minute Reflection Prompt:
- What is one way I can deepen a relationship in my life today?

1-Minute Scripture Focus:
- "Let all that you do be done in love." – 1 Corinthians 16:14

Reflect on how love strengthens and sustains relationships.

1-Minute Personal Prayer:
- Father, thank You for the relationships You've blessed me with. Teach me to nurture them with patience, honesty, and grace. Let my connections grow stronger as they reflect Your love and bring glory to You. Amen.

Daily Gratitude & Praise Prompt:
- "I showed love in my relationships today by ____."

Whisper Prayer:
- "Help me love deeply and sincerely."

16. Stepping Out in Faith: Prayers for Meeting New People

1-Minute Reflection Prompt:
- What is one way I can step out of my comfort zone and connect with someone new today?

1-Minute Scripture Focus:
- "For we live by faith, not by sight." – 2 Corinthians 5:7

Reflect on how stepping out in faith opens doors for meaningful connections.

1-Minute Personal Prayer:
- Lord, thank You for the opportunity to meet new people. Give me the courage to step out of my comfort zone and build meaningful connections. Help me approach new relationships with openness and trust in Your guidance. Amen.

Daily Gratitude & Praise Prompt:
- "I built a new connection today by ____."

Whisper Prayer:
- "Guide me to new connections, Lord."

17. A Helping Hand: Prayers for Supporting Others in Need

1-Minute Reflection Prompt:
- What is one way I can serve or support someone in need today?

1-Minute Scripture Focus:
- "Carry each other's burdens, and in this way, you will fulfill the law of Christ." – Galatians 6:2

Reflect on how God calls you to help others with love and compassion.

1-Minute Personal Prayer:
- Dear God, thank You for the chance to be Your hands and feet. Show me how to serve and support those in need today. Give me the strength and willingness to act, and let my actions reflect Your love. Amen.

Daily Gratitude & Praise Prompt:
- "I helped someone today by ____."

Whisper Prayer:
- "Show me who needs my help today."

18. Healing the Hurt: Prayers for Letting Go of Resentment

1-Minute Reflection Prompt:
- What is one hurt or resentment I can release to God today?

1-Minute Scripture Focus:
- "Get rid of all bitterness, rage and anger, brawling and slander, along with every form of malice." – Ephesians 4:31

Reflect on how God's grace empowers you to let go of pain and bitterness.

1-Minute Personal Prayer:
- Lord, holding onto resentment weighs heavy on my heart. Help me release the pain and embrace forgiveness, just as You have forgiven me. Heal the wounds of my past and restore peace to my spirit. Amen.

Daily Gratitude & Praise Prompt:
- "I found peace today by letting go of ____."

Whisper Prayer:
- "Free me from bitterness, Lord."

19. Celebrating Together: Prayers for Joyful Relationships

1-Minute Reflection Prompt:
- What is one moment of joy or celebration I can thank God for today?

1-Minute Scripture Focus:
- "Rejoice with those who rejoice; mourn with those who mourn." – Romans 12:15

Reflect on how shared joy strengthens relationships and honors God.

1-Minute Personal Prayer:
- God, thank You for the joy that comes from shared moments with loved ones. Help me to celebrate others with a heart full of gratitude and love, bringing glory to You in all we do. Amen.

Daily Gratitude & Praise Prompt:
- "I celebrated with others today by _____."

Whisper Prayer:
- "Thank You for shared joy and laughter."

20. God at the Center: Prayers for Spirit-Led Connections

1-Minute Reflection Prompt:
- What is one way I can keep God at the center of my relationships today?

1-Minute Scripture Focus:
- "Above all, love each other deeply because love covers over a multitude of sins." – 1 Peter 4:8

Reflect on how God's love strengthens and sustains every connection.

1-Minute Personal Prayer:
- Lord, thank You for being the foundation of my relationships. Help me to keep You at the center, guiding my words and actions with Your Spirit. May my relationships reflect Your love and grace. Amen.

Daily Gratitude & Praise Prompt:
- "I kept God at the center of my relationships today by__."

Whisper Prayer:
- "Be at the center of my relationships, Lord."

21. Patience in Differences: Prayers for Understanding Others

1-Minute Reflection Prompt:
- What is one situation today where I need God's help to practice patience with someone's differences?

1-Minute Scripture Focus:
- "Be completely humble and gentle; be patient, bearing with one another in love." – Ephesians 4:2

Reflect on how God calls us to respond with humility and love in all relationships.

1-Minute Personal Prayer:
- Lord, help me to be patient and understanding when I encounter differences in others. Teach me to listen with an open heart and see others through Your eyes. Let patience and grace guide my relationships, reflecting Your love. Amen.

Daily Gratitude & Praise Prompt:
- "I practiced patience today by ____."

Whisper Prayer:
- "Help me show patience and love."

22. Boundaries with Grace: Prayers for Protecting Healthy Relationships

1-Minute Reflection Prompt:
- What is one boundary I need to establish or respect in my relationships today?

1-Minute Scripture Focus:
- "Above all else, guard your heart, for everything you do flows from it." – Proverbs 4:23

Reflect on how God calls us to protect our hearts and relationships with wisdom and grace.

1-Minute Personal Prayer:
- God, thank You for teaching me the value of boundaries. Help me to establish and respect them with grace, protecting my peace and nurturing healthy relationships. Remind me that saying "no" with love is honoring You. Amen.

Daily Gratitude & Praise Prompt:
- "I protected my peace today by ____."

Whisper Prayer:
- "Help me guard my heart wisely."

23. Joy in Togetherness: Prayers for Strengthening Community Bonds

1-Minute Reflection Prompt:
- What is one moment of togetherness in my community that I can thank God for today?

1-Minute Scripture Focus:
- "How good and pleasant it is when God's people live together in unity!" – Psalm 133:1

Reflect on how unity and joy in the community are gifts from God.

1-Minute Personal Prayer:
- Lord, thank You for the joy of being part of a community. Help me to cherish the bonds of togetherness and nurture relationships with love and encouragement. May our time together bring glory to You. Amen.

Daily Gratitude & Praise Prompt:
- "I brought joy to my community today by ____."

Whisper Prayer:
- "Thank You for the joy of unity."

24. Speaking Life: Prayers for Words That Build Up

1-Minute Reflection Prompt:
- What is one conversation where I can choose words that bring life and encouragement today?

1-Minute Scripture Focus:
- "Gracious words are a honeycomb, sweet to the soul and healing to the bones." – Proverbs 16:24

Reflect on how kind and truthful words can uplift others.

1-Minute Personal Prayer:
- Dear Lord, guide my words today. Help me to speak with kindness, truth, and grace, building up those around me. May my words bring encouragement and hope, reflecting Your love in every conversation. Amen.

Daily Gratitude & Praise Prompt:
- "I used my words to uplift someone today by ____."

Whisper Prayer:
- "Let my words bring life and healing."

25. Overcoming Loneliness: Prayers for Finding Connection

1-Minute Reflection Prompt:
- What is one way God has reminded me today that I am never alone?

1-Minute Scripture Focus:
- "The Lord is close to the brokenhearted and saves those who are crushed in spirit." – Psalm 34:18

Reflect on God's constant presence and love, even in moments of loneliness.

1-Minute Personal Prayer:
- Lord, thank You for always being near. Help me overcome loneliness and guide me to connections that bring joy and encouragement. Remind me that I am never truly alone because You are always with me. Amen.

Daily Gratitude & Praise Prompt:
- "I found connection today by ____."

Whisper Prayer:
- "Thank You for Your comforting presence."

26. Gratitude for Friendship: Prayers for Cherishing Those Close to You

1-Minute Reflection Prompt:
- What is one way I can show appreciation for a friend in my life today?

1-Minute Scripture Focus:
- "Greater love has no one than this: to lay down one's life for one's friends." – John 15:13

Reflect on how friendship reflects God's love and sacrifice.

1-Minute Personal Prayer:
- Heavenly Father, thank You for the gift of friendship. Help me to cherish and nurture these relationships with love and care. May I never take my friends for granted, and may my actions reflect my gratitude for them. Amen.

Daily Gratitude & Praise Prompt:
- "I cherished my friendships today by ____."

Whisper Prayer:
- "Thank You for the friends who bless my life."

27. Support in Trials: Prayers for Being There for Others

1-Minute Reflection Prompt:
- What is one way I can offer strength or comfort to someone in need today?

1-Minute Scripture Focus:
- "Carry each other's burdens, and in this way, you will fulfill the law of Christ." – Galatians 6:2

Reflect on how God calls us to support one another in love and compassion.

1-Minute Personal Prayer:
- God, thank You for the opportunity to be a source of strength for others. Help me to comfort and encourage those going through trials, reminding them of Your love and presence. Amen.

Daily Gratitude & Praise Prompt:
- "I supported someone today by ____."

Whisper Prayer:
- "Help me carry someone's burden today."

28. Unity in Diversity: Prayers for Bridging Cultural Gaps

1-Minute Reflection Prompt:
- What is one way I can embrace and celebrate the diversity around me today?

1-Minute Scripture Focus:
- "Make every effort to keep the unity of the Spirit through the bond of peace." – Ephesians 4:3

Reflect on how unity and understanding glorify God in diversity.

1-Minute Personal Prayer:
- Lord, thank You for the beauty in diversity. Help me to see differences as opportunities for growth and connection. Teach me to embrace others with love and work toward unity that honors You. Amen.

Daily Gratitude & Praise Prompt:
- "I bridged a gap today by ____."

Whisper Prayer:
- "Thank You for the richness of diversity."

29. Hope for Restoration: Prayers for Rekindling Lost Relationships

1-Minute Reflection Prompt:
- What is one relationship in my life that I can pray for restoration today?

1-Minute Scripture Focus:
- "He restores my soul; He leads me in paths of righteousness for His name's sake." – Psalm 23:3

Reflect on God's power to heal and restore broken relationships.

1-Minute Personal Prayer:
- Father, thank You for being a God of restoration. Help me to rekindle lost relationships with forgiveness, grace, and

hope. Guide my heart and theirs toward healing and reconciliation. Amen.

Daily Gratitude & Praise Prompt:
- "I worked toward restoring a relationship today by ____."

Whisper Prayer:
- "Restore what has been broken, Lord."

30. Trust in God's Timing: Prayers for Waiting on the Right Connections

1-Minute Reflection Prompt:
- What is one way I can trust God's timing in my relationships today?

1-Minute Scripture Focus:
- "There is a time for everything and a season for every activity under the heavens." – Ecclesiastes 3:1

Reflect on how God's timing is perfect and purposeful.

1-Minute Personal Prayer:
- Lord, thank You for the reminder that Your timing is always perfect. Help me to trust You as I wait for the right connections in my life. Teach me to find peace in the waiting, knowing that You are working for my good. Amen.

Daily Gratitude & Praise Prompt:
- "I trusted God's timing today by ____."

Whisper Prayer:
- "Help me trust Your perfect timing, Lord."

www.ingramcontent.com/pod-product-compliance
Lightning Source LLC
LaVergne TN
LVHW011948060526
838201LV00061B/4246